More Tracks

78 Years of Mountains, People & Happiness

By Howard Copenhaver

Le Roy if life is as good to you as it has been to me I'll be happy

Howard
1993

More Tracks

78 Years of Mountains, People & Happiness

Copyright 1992 by Howard Copenhaver

ISBN 0912299-49-5 (Hardcover)
ISBN 0912299-50-9 (Softcover)

DEDICATION

This book is fondly dedicated to all people with family values.

All Rights Reserved

STONEYDALE PRESS PUBLISHING COMPANY
205 Main Street — Drawer B
Stevensville, Montana 59870
Phone: 406-777-2729

TABLE OF CONTENTS

FOREWORD

This is Howard's second book. I was around for Howard's first book, too, and I'll tell you about it in a bit. This second book is like the first book only more so.

I first met Howard some years ago, in the old Trixi's Saloon in Ovando. I was helping Hugo Eck with some task or another, for Hugo and Dorothy were making the building over into a museum. One of the exhibits was a pair of Howard's boots, artfully repaired with duct tape. I think Howard stopped by to see how we were treating his boots. He had a cast on one arm and various dings and abrasions on his person. He had been working some young horses, and there are hazards in messing around with animals that weigh a half-ton and have brains the size of raisins.

"What are these?" Hugo asked, holding up what seemed to be a brassiere designed for a midget.

"Bucking rolls," said Howard. Bucking rolls tie onto the saddle either side of the saddlehorn, to provide something for the rider's thighs to grip.

Well, I was introduced to Howard and for several quiet years after that I would pass Howard on the not very busy streets of Ovando and I would say "Hi, Mr. Copenhaver." We even committed conversation once or twice.

Even then I suppose the urge to write was festering in Howard. One wintry morning when he had nothing better to do he came to my door and there was a fearful pounding and bellering and when I opened it there was my neighbor, looking somewhat wrought.

"I want to write a book and I don't know how," he said.

"You're very lucky," I said, starting to close the door. He took a dive at the narrowing crack and soon we were having coffee. He pried some suggestions out of me and scurried off.

Now, normally folks listen to my suggestions, go back home and do nothing at all. Not Howard. Oh, no. He went back home and *wrote* a *book*. It was a good book, which was bad enough, but he had spasms of the gratefuls and told anyone who'd listen that I had made that very book possible. I hadn't felt this guilty since the hogs ate little sister, while I watched.

Early this year Howard called me.

"I wrote another book," he said.

I started to make thin, tearing noises deep in my throat.

"You got to read it by next Tuesday. I'm in a hurry," he went on.

I began to protest loudly, but Howard has mastered a new skill—that of turning off his hearing aid. (I am now writing this foreword by *this* Tuesday.) So I read his second book, which is very good.

"So write a third," I said, feeling vengeful, "old, established writers such as yourself have an obligation to provide example and inspiration to young and struggling writers such as myself. Also there are a lot of good stories in you which I propose to steal."

I could hear him grinning over the telephone.

So here they are, a second book of his memories. Howard tells us much in them, for he has lived much, and remembered it all. Unlike the pitiable cooked-pinky efforts of our literary sorts, there are real and important matters talked of here. His storytelling style is his and the West's.

I feel lucky to have known this .... fine......................gentleman.

Peter Bowen
Livingston, Montana
June 1992

MONTANA FIRST

How many times have you heard the old saying, "Montana, High, Wide and Handsome?" Did you ever wonder just what this means? Well, I'm going back a long time in history and explain it.

The first white men that came here saw wide grassy prairies, beautiful rivers leading up to the snow capped Rocky Mountains, and deep, lush valleys of the western slopes all covered by the "Big Sky"—so big and blue that at night you feel you can reach out and grab a handful of stars from around a moon so close. She could only inspire desire, ambition and dignity to all who live here. One couldn't help but be inspired by the wealth and splendor here to be shared by all.

The first settlers here could have had their pick of prairie, high mountains or low valleys, of climate mild enough to raise anything from wheat to cherry blossomed fruit trees, to settle in and make a home.

Her rolling grasslands and snow-capped mountains, rivers and valleys were covered with buffalo, elk, deer, antelope, Rocky Mountain bighorn sheep, Rocky Mountain goat, moose, mountain lion, black and grizzly bear, along with wolves and many other species of smaller game and wildlife.

Buffalo and the furbearing beaver brought the mountain men and trappers, along with the buffalo hunters, in search of wealth. She gave us the greatest fur country of the world, long fought over by the Indians, trappers and England's Hudson Bay Fur Trading Company.

Gold, silver and copper then brought the miners. She gave us Last Chance Gulch, Virginia City and Bannack, so rich in gold and history, Granite with the richest silver mine in the world and copper from Butte, "The Richest Hill on Earth." It was here that F. Augustus Heinze, W. A. Clark and Marcus Daly fought for financial control in the "War of the Copper Kings."

Danaher Valley

Then the Fort Union Coal deposit in eastern Montana is still a big source of income supporting education in the state of Montana.

The lumber industry from her heavy forested hills and valleys has bolstered the economy for her many people.

We get millions of gallons of crude oil and natural gas from her underground storage tanks on her high plains and Rocky Mountain front.

When it comes to agriculture, thousands of cattle, sheep and horses graze the lands once covered with buffalo. Many thousands of acres of golden grain waving in the breeze make Montana one of the food baskets of the world.

Wildlife has been a great part of her gift to the world. Today she can boast she is the only state in the Lower 48 that still produces every kind of wild animal ranging her hills and valleys that ever was here to greet the first white man, and they are still in abundance today.

Now, as my mother always used to quote when things got tough and all looked glum, "I look up into the hills from whence cometh my help." I am sure what inspired Montana's many talented people came from what they saw around them. They may not have been artists or authors of such great value without it. She is still giving in most all that she had at first. Many have become nationally and worldly known.

Charles Russell painted many pictures of biographical value of Indian life and history of the open range cattle era and cowboy life in Montana. His most famous painting, the mural "Lewis and Clark Meeting

Montana gold.

the Flathead Indians," adorns the wall of the House of Representatives in our State Capitol. A pen and ink sketch, "Waiting for a Chinook," or "The Last of the 5000," proclaimed the end of the open range cattle business caused by the extreme winter of 1888. He also wrote of the historical development of the state in a book titled, "Trails Plowed Under."

There also is A. B. Guthrie and his Pulitzer Prize winning book, "The Way West," and "The Big Sky," a novel of the mountain man era.

Also Ace Powell, sculptor and artist, brought to life Indian culture and wildlife of the west.

Montana also gave us some of Hollywood's finest actors—Helena native Gary Cooper, who had a home at Wolf Creek and Myrna Loy of Radersburg, to top the list.

Statesmen or politicians, call them what you choose. I could name many from Montana who have won national acclaim but will name just a few.

Number one is Jeannette Rankin. She was the first woman in Congress and the only one to vote against World War I and World War II. She did much for women's suffrage.

Mike Mansfield served his state well in both education and as a Senate Majority Leader of the U. S. Senate, retiring as U. S. Ambassador to Japan.

Montana has given herself to sports—producing many a world champion.

What the glaciers left.

We will start with world class biathlete Kari Swenson.

Then track. Greg Rice of Missoula, long distance runner of the 1930's and '40's.

Rodeo. Fanny Sperry Steele, undefeated world champion lady bronc rider of 1912 and the famous 101 Wild West Show of William F. "Wild Bill" Cody. In the men's division, the famous names like Greenough, Linderman, Reynolds, and Ingersoll. There are too many to list all the riders who won world championships. The same goes with authors and people of art. There are so many I only mention a few well-known.

Now, here's a horse of a different color. Montana is the only state that bought a train, rebuilt it and furnished it, loaded it with seventy-five head of horses and mules, stagecoach, wagons, Tallyhos with cowboys, outfitters, native tribal Indian dancers, a million dollars of raw gold in display cars, along with western art and artifacts and toured the eastern cities to advertise what she has. We paraded fourteen of the largest cities east of the Mississippi River, ending up opening the 1964 World's Fair in New York City with our "Centennial Train," pavilion and parade.

There were 306 Montanans who paid their own way on that train just to show people what Montana has. The ages of these people ran from

Marg and I in Baltimore.

close to 100 years old down to young men and women in their early teens. Show me a state that's done more!

The year following our advertising raised the visitors to Yellowstone and Glacier National Parks to over two million people, by extending our hospitality and showing them what Montana has through pictures and conversation. Our tourist trade in Montana is now the number two industry in the state. These thousands of people come to take home with them nothing but what they can see.

It is hard to realize the money spent to just have a look-see at what we see every day. It is kind of like the little boy standing in the forest and his dad asked him what he thought of the forest. His answer, "I can't see the forest. There are too many trees."

From here on I will try to show you what Montana has shared with me, or more rightly, has given to me in its people, mountains, rivers and prairies—a life of hope, happiness and dignity just by allowing me to be a part of her people.

Ovando from the air.

MY MOUNTAIN

As I lay here in my sleeping bag on top of "My Mountain", Scapegoat, a huge pile of rocks and crags that support the Continental Divide, backbone of Montana, I look as far as the eye will allow me East, North, South and West. It is not hard to visualize dreams of the past. Off to the southeast I see Lewis and Clark trudging up the Missouri headed for the Pacific. I see Indians chasing buffalo or a Blackfoot Indian war party in search of the Crow Indians. A little farther north and east is Charlie Russell and a group of cowboys raising a dust as they head for the "Old Mint" bar in Great Falls. What's that streak across the plains? It's a homesteader and his plow. Right behind him comes a mangy crew planting post and barbed wire. I can see cattle grazing through the tall prairie grass with sheep climbing the foothills in search of feed. Elk, deer, goat, mountain sheep and grizzly bear looking down the mountain and wondering, "How long can I hold my ground?" Farther north stands the Anaconda Smelter at Great Falls, a city that covers the prairie like ringworm on a horse's eye.

Off to the west and far below I see fertile valleys, lakes and streams, ranches and cities, sawmills and loggers with logging roads. Also, farther south, mines of silver and copper and gold. Off to the side is the "Richest Hill on Earth," the mines of Butte. I dream I can hear the clatter of trains when I'm rudely awakened out of my trance by the roar of a Boeing 707 jet as it flies overhead.

I've tried to tell people of this and more. Always their comment to me has been, "If only this mountain could talk!"

I'm going to lay here and listen and take down some notes, maybe she'll have something to say of days long gone by and years to come. I'll try to write them all down and pass them on. Then you'll know she's something that lives and man can't change.

My Scapegoat Mountain.

She's a beautiful, spectacular mountain whose lifeblood (water) flows down her sides to head the great rivers. On the north flows the South Fork of the Flathead, to the west the North Fork of the Blackfoot. They flow on to the Pacific. To the east the Dearborn, Marias, Milk, Sun and Yellowstone rivers join the Missouri River, then flow into the great Mississippi all the way to the Atlantic Ocean. Scapegoat is a name taken out of the Bible so why shouldn't she stand high and stately over all the other mountains reigning as queen!

Well, I'm getting sleepy. I think I'll have the last of that coffee and turn in. It's a beautiful night. I can almost touch the stars and that moon is so bright I can see like day.

"What did you say? Hey, there's no one here." I must be dreaming.

"Oh, yes, there's someone here alright. It's me, the mountain. You lay still and listen. I'll tell you of my past as best I can.

"Many millions of years ago I was the flat bottom of the ocean. I can prove it by the many seashells and fossils of fish and horned sharks imbedded in my stony face. Then a great change came and I became a prehistoric tropical plain with dense swamps and lush tropical plains bordered by a sea whose shores were lined with pine and redwood forests.

These lands and swamps were inhabited by dinosaurs, large and small. There were the Triassic, the Jurassic and the Cretaceous.

Then we mountains started to grow. As we raised our heads up, the water receded, drying up the swamps and changing all vegetation and climate as well. We grew until we towered many thousands of feet high forming the backbone of America, the Continental Divide.

"Then came the Ice Age with its glaciers shifting, tearing at our sides. They slipped, leaving beautiful cirques, plateaus and canyons along with the Great China Wall. The earth heaved and buckled. How long this lasted I do not know. When it was all done, there was a great dam way off to the west somewhere near where Thompson Falls now is, causing a great lake. Lake Missoula was formed as the ice melted, raising the waters until they broke out and flooded the Columbia Basin and rushed to the Pacific Ocean below.

"If you drive down Highway 90 and stop near Missoula, the shoreline of Lake Missoula is clearly defined high on the sides of my sisters, Mount Jumbo and Mount Sentinel. All the valleys to the west are lake beds of washed gravel and rocks washed smooth, covered with sedimentation that has now become soil.

"Great forests of pine, fir, spruce and larch have covered our sidehills, valleys and ridges. Grasses, bushes, willows, berries, cottonwood and aspen trees are here for the use of animals, birds and man. (To the north, south and west you'll see great forests of trees 200 feet high.)

"As it was, you'd find Indians on both sides of this mountain. To the west were the Nez Perce and Flathead. Out east were the Crow and to the north the Blackfeet with the Cree in between. They are hunting and fishing in a land that is free. Sure, they fought over areas, but, in all, it was a good life. There's plenty of room to wander and enjoy a good life. Then here come the trappers and mountain men, and also the searchers for gold. Soon the cattlemen and farmers followed.

"You ask me where did all the animals come from? I really don't know. I hear they walked across land or ice bridges from Russia and Asia and maybe Finland or Sweden. Your guess is as good as mine but I think The Great Spirit, God, put them here.

"I can prove all I've told you if you'll just look below. To the east they are digging out dinosaur fossils over 60 million years old. Right at my feet they've found huge fossils along the Sun River and even dinosaur eggs. Right now they are digging up Tyrannosaurus Rex that is supposed to be 65 million years old. This is to the east on the Missouri River Breaks. Just below me on Wolf Creek is a cave on Tag Rittell's ranch. They are finding fossils and bones of animals many thousands of years old, also, a skull of prehistoric man, so they claim."

"Hold it right here, Old Friend, you've lost me. Can I ask you some questions as we go along?

"What of the Hudson Bay Fur Company traders who came across the plains to the Missouri and Marias Rivers to set up fur trading posts with the Cree and the Blackfoot Indians? When I was quite young, some prospectors came to us. They wanted us to pack them and their equipment in to the head of the Dry Fork in search of gold and any traces left by these Hudson Bay men. They had documents claiming a strike that these men had made; also a crude map of how they travelled. They came up from the prairie to Half Moon Park, then off to the north and up that long ridge between Green Creek and Straight Creek, climbed up on top where they found gold in soft quartz. They needed water to wash it so they packed it down into the Dry Fork to the west. Here they made sluice boxes out of hued logs. Then they went back over the top and down to the plains. They did not cut blazes on trees to mark their trail—they built monuments of stone and on your west face they painted the Royal British Shield. We packed them into the Dry Fork where they spent two summers. When I packed them out that last summer, they showed me their find—no gold or quartz left around. Just the rotten old sluice boxes hued out of fir logs where the creek had washed gravel and rocks over them many years ago. This story goes, that on the second trip, when they hit the plains south of Great Falls on their way home, the Blackfeet Indians overtook them. When the dust settled on this skirmish, they had no gold and no hair!

Deep in the wilderness.

"While hunting mountain goat years after this I found three different places where someone had painted the British Shield on the cliffs facing west at the foot of the Cabin Creek Reef."

"I cannot answer you, my son, but I can tell you someone built piles of stone marking a trail and painted my face with that old British Shield. Daylight is approaching and it's time for me to go. Write down your experiences, my friend, so others might know of your love for the mountains, animals and fellow man."

From up here with nothing to do but think, my mind gets to running away. I've seen so many big years of advancement I could never put it all in one book—gas-powered carriages, diesel motors, radio, flying machines to supersonic jets. Now, men on the moon and weapons so accurate you can pinpoint a target miles out of your sight.

There is also television and laser light even used for bloodless operations.

Then there's this do-hickey that doctors use where they can see inside of you to tell what ails you.

This has most all happened in less than my lifetime of 78 years. Have I had a full life? You can bet I have!

This all makes me feel I must be one special guy for the Lord to have let me live through this period and have such a wonderful memory of the past.

My memory takes me back to my childhood days and so I write.

A fancy car, 1915

A remodeled soddy.

HOMESTEAD DAYS

It must have been along about 1911 or '12 that my father and some other young fellows from Washington State came to Montana to check on ground open to homesteading. This area laid north of Great Falls and east of Brady. They took up claims in the area 22 miles east of Brady, just west of Lytle Coulee.

This was a wide open cattle country then. The Matador Cattle Ranch on the Missouri and Marias rivers to the east and the Texarkana Cattle Ranch on the Teton River, were both unfriendly to the "Sod Busters" or homesteaders. Any crops the homesteaders raised had to be fenced mighty solid. Now this didn't always help much. I can remember my folks had 80 acres of wheat fenced in when along came the Texarkana cowboys with a large herd of cattle, cut the fence and drove the cattle into the grain field. There was no reason to cut the grain. The cows did a good job. This was common practice at first 'til the homesteaders became thicker and more organized. In later years the cowmen became friendlier and backed off, leaving the homesteaders to become wheat ranchers, raising thousands of acres of golden grain. I have many fond memories of those days on the homestead and shortly afterwards.

How people survived those days is a mystery to me. Except for a strong-willed desire and lots of "Just Plain Guts" they'd have all quit even trying. I can remember the rattlesnakes, Army worms and grasshoppers by the millions. It looked as if the ground itself was moving toward you as they came from west to east. If you left a pitchfork or shovel outside overnight they would eat the wooden handles, fence posts, grain, gardens and grass. It was all gone when they passed through the country. The years before they came everybody had sixty to seventy bushels per acre wheat and lots of Buffalo grass.

There are lighter spots in my mind though. We had to haul all our water four miles from down on the Teton River. We had big water tanks

Horsepower on homestead.

on high-wheeled wagons drawn by four to six head of horses. When the men went to haul water all us kids would ride along. While the men were filling the tank with water, us kids would go swimming and fishing. Sometimes there would be a number of neighbors hauling water the same day. When this happened there would be a picnic lunch by the ladies and the men would bring a fish net. Five or six men would spread the net out between them and walk through the deeper holes in the river in a half circle motion, dragging the net between them. When they came to the edge of the hole they would drag the net and fish out on the rocks. We would all dive in picking the big fish and throwing the smaller ones back in the river. Sometimes we would have a washtub full of fish. You'd have goldeyes, pike, ling, catfish and sometimes a trout or two. The fish would be divided and everyone went home with enough water for a week, used for domestic use only. Cattle, horses and other livestock used the water in the sloughs or little lakes and reservoirs built to catch rain or snow water.

Most ranchers dug cisterns. These were big holes in the ground lined with cement and a tight lid on top. The water tank was backed up to the cistern and the water dumped into it. This would keep the water relatively cool and clean. You'd dip the water as needed with a bucket with a rope on the handle. Once in a while someone would not secure the lid well and you'd find lizards or ground squirrels in the water the next day. We'd have to dip them out. Sometimes this ran into quite a job as lizards can sure swim fast, but it didn't seem to hurt the water as we all lived.

Heading grain.

Everywhere you went it was either by saddle horse, wagon or buckboard. The buckboard was a glorified pickup at that time as it was light and pulled by light horses and a faster mode of travel. Also, if you had the money you could have a beautiful spring seat on the front. Only the driver and a chosen two could ride on it though. All kids sat on the floor in back. Some people had buggies. These were the Cadillacs of the time. They had two seats and a top, also some had side curtains with celluloid windows you could see out of. No rain, snow or wind to fight. Us kids always figured those people must have been millionaires. When someone came to visit with one of these, we'd set in it and play we were driving it with a beautiful team going at least 100 miles an hour.

We lived in a sod house built by my father and his friends. I can still see my mother doing her best to keep the house clean with the wind blowing dust or snow through the places not sealed well around the door and windows, wetting down the dirt floor and sweeping it to cause the clay to set up hard on the surface. Finally Dad got a couple of bucks ahead and bought some lumber in Brady, hauled it home and built another room onto the old soddy. He also laid a floor of wood in the old part of the house. What a castle! The only trouble was that the rattlesnakes took up housekeeping under our new floor.

According to us boys we had two unneeded improvements come to the country about this time. One was a cowboy preacher who rode through the country stopping at everybody's place and having devotional services. I for one should and could have listened and accepted it far better than I did. Today I can see this but then I could see only his horse and saddle with me chasing cows over the prairie, swinging a rope and smoking a Bull Durham cigarette—plumb the wrong attitude. Then there came this country doctor with his pills, salves and that vaccine and a square needle about fourteen inches long. I know for sure.

About this time diphtheria and smallpox was showing up all over the country so the good doctor was making the rounds of homesteaders and ranches vaccinating all the kids. When he hit our place he started in on the oldest. Leona, my sister, was first. Bless her heart, she took it without a word. Gene, my brother was next. He didn't do so well. About the first squawk out of him and I was gone like a scairt rabbit. I crawled under the new addition to the house and up between the sod and wood framing where no man could reach me. After much threatening and coaxing, my Dad sent Gene under the house and after me. He got a hold of my leg and pulled me down where my Dad could reach me and he pulled me out from under the house. This is how I can verify the length of that square needle. I have always claimed they threatened Gene with a double shot of that needle if he didn't crawl under the house and git me. Well, "All's well that ends well," I guess, cause I didn't get diphtheria.

They built a school house off across the prairie to the west about a mile and a half from our place. My sister, Leona, and brother, Gene, started school over there. They would walk to and from each day.

Now the Texarkana Ranch had this big dapple grey stallion running loose on the range with some mares, raising horses. He was "German Coach" as I remember but a beautiful animal and as mean as a snake. If he saw the kids walking to or from school he'd take after them and would have killed them if they didn't get through a fence or hide someplace. Once they crawled in a badger hole.

My Dad and uncles caught him one day, roping him and throwing him. I think this is where a little bit of my cowboy nature came from. They wired a five gallon oil can to his tail, put a handful of small rocks in the can and then turned him loose, sicking the dogs on him and chasing him east toward home. You should have seen him go kicking at the can and jumping in the air. It was nine or ten miles across the prairie to the Knees, two high square buttes rising out of the prairie. The last we saw of that stud horse was the sun shining on the can when it flew up in the air. No one ever saw that stallion again. Mebby that's where they got such good horses up in Canada.

About this time, everyone was talking about this new rig they called a Model T Ford. Grandpa Edwards bought one and my uncle, Dan, drove it home and down to our place. What a beautiful thing! Jet black with brass headlights, a top you could let down and side curtains with windows in them. Oh, what a great thing to just sit in it on those beautiful leather seats with padding in them and rubber tires all around. It also had a big rubber round thing that you squeezed and it blew a horn. Oh, what fun until we were shagged out and made to get in only when we were asked to.

My first trip in this machine, that I can remember, was to Genou. Someone was putting on a moving picture show. Uncle Dan picked up the whole family and away we went. What a thrill! All my life this first movie has remained as one of the greatest things that ever was invented.

First, they hung a bed sheet on the schoolhouse wall, then put blankets over all the windows. One guy set up a tripod with a big black thing on top. Another guy put a strong light behind it and a black cover over him and the projector. Then the other guy turned a crank and on the sheet came this writing and pictures. Now us kids had seen a funny paper or two so we knew the characters when they came on the sheet. It was Mutt and Jeff and they were painting on a skyscraper in Chicago or New York. What a time they had! As they came by a window Jeff saw a woman in a bathtub and quit pulling on his end of the rope holding the scaffold and he and Mutt and the paint went in the window right into the bathtub where the woman was taking a bath. You can talk about sending up "Space Ships." That's small potatoes compared to what us kids thought of the movies we saw that night. Mutt and Jeff and Maggie and Jiggs! What an unbelievable feat. Of all memories in my mind for over seventy years, this still remains most vivid. One never knows what small things will impress a young mind so vivid and lasting.

Grampa's Ford.

Along came World War I and many of the young men joined to fight for freedom. Some came back. Among the first, an uncle and a guy by the name of Bill Hopkins. When they arrived home they had two wooden rifles for me and my brother, our first guns. These were wooden guns used in Army training. I shall never forget them.

Oh, yes, I almost forgot about Montgomery Ward and Co. My mother would order boxes of dried apples, pears and peaches, along with shoes, etc. Monkey Ward was a standby shopping mall. Even the old catalogs were used in the outhouse, sometimes not lasting the year around. Anyway the dried fruit was the only source of fruit in those days. Us boys would get into these boxes every once in a while and steal some dried fruit. Mom would give us a real going over and force all kinds of punishment on us but to no avail.

One day she caught me red-handed in the dried apples. She says, "Come with me." She got a teacup full of dried apples and another full of water. "Now," she says, "you eat all of those apples." Me, I think this is a joke on her. So I ate the apples. "Now, you drink this water." I'll admit I needed a drink at this time but not so much. Those apples started to swell and my belly started to swell and you talk about a bellyache. It was the real thing. I was hurting and Mom was scared and tried to make me vomit them up but they just swelled up more. She made me run, bend over, jump up and down. Well, finally the swelling went down. Now that night she was telling Dad about it and she said, "I'll never do that again!" I didn't say anything but I knew I'd never eat dried apples again, stolen or otherwise.

One night the folks were talking about the war days and my uncle, Dan, says, "You know the Chinese people don't have much beef so when they get some meat to eat, each one is given a small piece of meat and a string tied to it. They swallow the meat and pull it up every once in a while, then swallow it again. That way they have beef steak for several days." Next day Gene and me decided we'll try this out. Mom says, "No, if you want to try this you tie the string to a piece of bread and tie the other end to your finger so you can pull the string back." Well, we did this and she made us go outside as she knew we'd heave. We couldn't get the string to go down, so Gene says, "Let's put the string and bread in our mouth, then take a drink of water." I watched as he did this. Nothing to it. But when he went to pull the string out, it gagged him and he'd heave. By the time he had half the string out, I'd decided the Chinese could have this. I never saw so many tears and so much heaving from one guy in my life. When the string was finally retrieved my Mother and uncle were almost sick with laughter. We sure found out research is a great thing to try before you experiment with Oriental tricks.

Another deal that happened about this time I call "The birth of a

Hauling grain to Brady, Montana.

cowboy." All the farmers had a few cows running on the range. Every spring they'd round them up and everybody'd help each other brand, etc., all the calves. One time all the cattle were corralled east of our grandparent's place. Between the corral and the buildings was an old lake bed with about four to six inches of water in it. From the corrals to the buildings was about a quarter of a mile.

When the men would finish branding a calf one of us boys would jump on him and try our luck at riding. We sure got dumped a lot. Finally, my brother Gene and the Golahon boys, our cousins, decided my legs were not strong enough to grip the calf's body. So, after they had branded a pet calf belonging to our milk cow, Gene and Leon held the calf while Hillary tied my feet together under the calf. When all was set they turned Ole Snowball loose. I done fine just like a top bronc peeler until I slipped sideways and I was underneath and Snowball on top. Well, Snowball figured he should head for the barn and he sure did. One jump on the ground and two jumps on me clear across that lake bottom. Mom and my grandmother saw us coming and ran out and caught old Snowball and cut me loose. I was out cold as a fish and just as wet. They shook me and hit me on the back for a while. I finally came around and have lived happily ever since—just better for the experience.

Then there was a bachelor who had a claim over west of our place. Parker was his name. He was over six feet tall and very slim. He worked more for other people than he did for himself. Now somewhere along the line of life he had lost his right eye. He wore a black patch over it with a rubber band around his head holding the patch in place. Whenever he would see us kids he'd jerk that patch off and take after us. We were scared to death of this man. We called him "One Eyed Parker" and figured he had to be some sort of a witch. We were always wondering where his broom was, as a witch has to have a broom. Nobody could convince us of anything else. I've even seen him in my dreams. This was back in 1917 or 1918.

Along in the winter of 1949 or 50, Marg, my wife, and I drove to New York City on a booking trip to book hunters and summer guests for the following season. Well, we stopped for gas in a small town in Illinois. After filling the car, I was just looking around and resting a bit when an elderly man came down the street. He had a cane and wasn't travelling very fast. Now, as he passed my car he sort of stopped and took another look at the license plate. Then he turned around and hobbled up to me and says, "From Montana, huh?" I said, "Yes." And he said "I had a brother who went out to Montana years ago. Took up some homestead land near a town or post office called Lytle." I says, "What was his name?" He said, "Parker. But we never heard from him again. I've often wondered what happened to him." The wheels started turning in my head and I said, "My folks had a homestead just west of Lytle and I was the first Copenhaver born in Montana in 1914. Now did this brother have only one eye?" He says, "That's him. He used to scare all of the kids around here by taking off the patch and chasing them."

We had a good visit but I knew nothing of what happened to One Eyed Parker. It made me realize just how small the world really is. After all those years in a strange place and two complete strangers meeting on such common ground.

Along about 1918 the hot winds and drought hit our country real hard. It had been real dry and very poor crops before. Nineteen eighteen and nineteen nineteen were the end of grass and crops. All the farmers went together and trailed all the horses, except those they had to have, to new pastures. It was across the prairie and over the mountains to the Blackfoot Valley and Ovando, over 200 miles to the Scotty Brown Ranch on the Big Blackfoot River west of Ovando. After the burned up prairie and from the stories they told, the Blackfoot must have looked like the Garden of Eden to them. Some never returned, but settled here. By this time the only people that stayed on the homesteads were those that owed the banks so much money that the banks wouldn't let them move. I'm sure my father never forgot the Blackfoot 'cause after trying other work such as managing a cattle ranch for the Birch Construction Company of Great Falls, working in a flour mill and a spell of tying steel and work in the Anaconda Copper Mining Company's wire mills in Great Falls, he rented a small ranch on the North Fork of the Blackfoot River and it has been home ever since. It is truly God's country with the wonderful people, the beauty of the valley and the open wilderness mountains and valleys from here to Glacier National Park, free for all to hunt, fish and enjoy. It is as close to Heaven as anywhere short of death.

Moving over the Continental Divide to our new home was quite an experience. We had an old truck and when we came to Alice Creek just east of Lincoln the ring gear and pinion went to pot. Here we sat in the middle of nowhere and the truck wouldn't move. Well, we pushed it off the road right along the creek and set up camp.

While our father went in search of repairs in Helena, we boys went fishing. We had willow poles with a short piece of line tied to it and plain hooks with grasshoppers for bait. Did we catch fish! All small but lots of them and a real treat to eat. We were camped there for several days when along came this guy in a Model T Ford and stopped for a visit. Lunch was ready so he was invited. After a meal of fried spuds and onions and fresh fish and coffee, he says, "I'm the game warden. My name is Harry Morgan. Did you see those red signs on that tree?" No we hadn't, but it was sure there alright. "It said NO FISHING, THIS STREAM CLOSED." By this time he knew of our troubles and where we were headed and he said, "I won't arrest you but when you boys want to fish, walk way up the creek where no one can see you from the road." This was our first education in game laws. A bunch of flatlanders, we learned in a hurry. I've always had a soft spot in my heart for Old Harry Morgan.

Up to this time I had never seen a deer or elk. I'd only been told about them, how beautiful they were and always they were seen in the trees (in timbered country.) So as we came on down the road across Kleinschmidt Flat and crossed the Ryan Bridge on the North Fork River everybody started yelling, "Look at the deer." I looked and looked but I couldn't see anything. Finally someone said, "Right in the middle of the road," and sure enough there, standing on the ground in the center of the road, was a whitetail doe. This was such a big disappointment to me because I thoroughly expected to see them perched up in a tree on a limb. I'd always wondered how a deer could climb a tree but had never connected a deer in the timber with a deer up a tree. Dreams exploded but still linger in your mind.

The ranch that Dad had leased was called the "Tait Place." It was owned by Dr. Tait, a dentist, who lived in Butte, Montana. When we arrived, what a beautiful spot, with one creek running by on each side of the house. Both creeks were full of fish, cutthroat and Dolly Varden. Lots of big ones with the Dollies up to twenty pounds, lots of cutthroat up to two or three pounds. Ducks and geese and big spruce, fir and pine trees scattered everywhere with meadows and grassland in between. A big log house with a fireplace that smoked till your eyes hurt but so beautiful to see the fire burning at night.

The big stack at Great Falls.

There was a fellow by the name of Tattoo Kelly living there taking care of things 'til we got there. He was a big man, six foot plus and probably 225 pounds. He was an ex-sailor and had tatoos all over his arms, hands, chest, and even on his back. He also was an alcoholic. Us kids had never been around anyone who drank before. We thought he was sure enough funny when drunk but this surely changed sudden-like when one day he came home from town and that night he got the snakes. He got his rifle off the wall and started shooting at the snakes he saw in his bedroom. Dad finally got his gun and poured some hot, strong coffee into him and sort of sobered him up. Now let me tell you he sure left a solid impression on some kids about strong drink that preaching could never do.

I know everyone has probably heard of Gypsies but to see and know them is something different. They were what you'd call nomads, I believe, never stayed long in any one place—always on the move. They travelled in family groups, had covered wagons and tents. Always they'd have a few horses and cows—ready for a trade with anyone who wanted to take a chance on a new horse, a stolen saddle or some other item. To say the least, they were a shady lot. There was always an older woman who could tell your fortune, even if you didn't have one, for a nominal fee. They were good gamblers and could sure shuffle the cards.

When a group of them came through Lewis and Clark County, the sheriff would call the Powell County sheriff, he'd call Granite County law and he'd call the Missoula sheriff so they could be on the lookout for them. If they stole too much in one area the deputies would usher them on to the next county.

Now some were fine and would stop and come near a town for a spell. They would sell all kinds of articles such as willow baskets and handmade tapestry, while the men ran games of chance, traded and if they could cook up a horse race they'd be happy. All of them had a race horse or two.

One such group stopped near Drummond, Montana. It was around the Fourth of July and on the Fourth there was to be a rodeo and horse races with all the outlying ranchers and communities taking part. There was at that time, four men around here who were excellent horsemen. One was a top bronc rider, another the best man with a rope I have ever seen, the other two were hard-working ranchers who loved a horse race. One of them owned this bay mare, a "thoroughbred," that could run like a scared rabbit. She could outrun anything in the valley. All of them worked hard and played the same way, loving a game of chance. Well, they were making wagers with this Gypsy and it looked good to them.

The night of the third, two of them were jawing with the Gypsy and keeping him occupied while the other two was stealing his race horse. Well, they took the Gypsy's horse out and had a race of their own that night on the county road. That Gypsy horse couldn't catch Bill's mare no matter how they ran them. Next day when the races began the Gypsies brought out their race horse and off went the race. Now this horse that couldn't outrun them the night before left Bill's bay mare like as if she was standing still. The Gypsy horse came in so far ahead that the Old Bay Mare didn't even know it was a race.

Well, the boys went over to pay their bets. This race had cleaned them of cash. When they were all settled up and shook hands—no hard feelings—this old Gypsy reached in his pockets and produced some horse shoes and said, "Now you boys might know your cows and horses but you don't know much about races." Now after one look at the shoes, my friends knew why that horse ran so slow the night before. Each shoe was lined with lead making them weigh about seven pounds apiece. This old Gypsy had figured what the boys were going to do and had shod the race horse the day before. The morning of the races he had pulled her shoes and ran her barefooted in the race. You couldn't beat those Gypsies with a baseball bat. I'm sure those weighted shoes had been used many times before.

There were many stories told and retold about them. How true they were is anybody's guess. For sure they were thieves. One story was what parents pounded into their kids' heads. They said the Gypsies would steal little kids and sell them into slavery where the owner would beat them and make them work awful hard. I don't know how true this was but you can believe kids took it for the truth.

Shocking bundles of grain.

Thirty-two head on a combine.

HARVEST TIME

There were hundreds of acres of grain to be cut each fall. At first we had binders that would cut and tie the grain in bundles about three feet long and fourteen inches in diameter. Then these would be either hauled in and stacked or shocked out in the field until threshing time. When you were ready to thresh, the threshing machine would be pulled in and all the neighbors would bring teams and wagons and haul the bundles to the machine.

Then there was the header. It cut only the top third of the grain, elevated it into a header box on a wagon driven alongside of the header. When the box was full you'd pull out to the stackyard and someone else would pull in alongside of the header chute while you stacked your load in a stackyard.

It was all pitchfork work with the men stacking several stacks to a place. When the grain was seasoned and ready to be threshed the threshing machine would be pulled in between the stacks and you'd pitch the grain into the machine from on top of the stacks. These headers were pulled by six to eight work horses.

Finally, someone invented the combine. It was a header and thresher all in one, a big heavy machine drawn by at least thirty-two horses, depending on how big the cutting bar was. In the accompanying picture, Dad is driving thirty-two head to pull this one.

While the machine was threshing, a Bull Tank was pulled alongside of the combine and the grain was elevated into the Bull Tank. When it was full, it was hauled to the granary or elevator in the town of Brady. The grain that was stored at home was then hauled to Brady in the winter time. So you always had a job either planting, harvesting or hauling grain the year round—no rest for the wicked.

A bumper crop.

Nowadays you hear people crying about how much diesel and gasoline cost them for tractors in the field. I wonder how costs would compare nowadays just to feed all those work horses because most farmers of any size had to keep forty to fifty of those old canners around just to farm their places, plus mend harness and equipment. At today's prices it would cost you around $180 to $200 a head just to feed one horse for a year. My calculator don't work that good.

HAYING TIME

Haying time was one of the big and busy times of the year when I was a young man. All of the ranchers did everything with teams. They would each have from three to eight or ten mowing machines cutting hay, three or four dump rakes, and two to mebby fourteen bullrakes or sweeps working in the fields. Then there would be the stackers stacking the hay. No one had balers or swathers then. It was all done with teams of horses. This brought a big need for teamsters and stackers.

Men following this kind of labor flocked to the valleys of western Montana from all over the United States and Canada. Some were good and some were not. We had men from college professors to railroad bums. All worked hard and played hard. I've seen on Saturday in both Ovando and Helmville, from forty to sixty strangers, all patronizing the local bars. There was plenty of moonshine and home brew for all.

One of these men that stands out in my memory is "Calgary Curly." He was as well-known as Rex, King of Tramps, a few years before his time. He was a huge man, over six feet tall and 200 pounds of muscle and bones. I never remember seeing him with a shirt and his torso, chest, shoulders and arms were covered with tattoos and huge knife scars. He sure loved a rough time, as well as lots of booze.

One Saturday night me and two friends were playing dance music in the old log dance hall in Ovando. Calgary and a bunch of hay hands were whooping it up in the "Bucket of Blood," run by a guy named Barbee. By the way, Barbee had a daughter. She was really something for the eyes. Her dresses barely covered her fanny and, if she was careful how she buttoned her blouse, it would almost do the same there. I'll tell you, she sure filled out them clothes. (Hey, I got off my story!)

Anyway, Old Calgary really pinned one on that night. He got sort of sleepy and laid down out in the town square in the middle of the road. Along about 2 o'clock or later, my friend Bill came into the dance hall, (he

Mowing hay horsepower.

was feeling no pain,) looking for help. It seemed he and his friend, Orville, drove into town in Orville's old Model T, both of them full of giggle juice. They couldn't see Old Curly taking his nap and ran right over him. Old Curly was so big the car frame rolled him along under it. When his body got close to the rear wheels, it lifted them off the ground and the boys were high centered on Curly, spinning their rear wheels.

Well, about six or seven of us went out there and lifted that Ford up and rolled it off of Curly. Bill and Orville climbed in and drove away. We dragged Curly over near the store and left him. The next morning he was just as good as new; he knew nothing about the trouble he'd caused.

One year, right in the middle of haying, a neighbor died. He was a very elderly gentleman, a real nice guy. My father donated Gene and me, along with two hay hands, to dig the grave. Now, you did this with a pick and shovel—no backhoes then. We set to work this morning but that ground was so dry and hard, just like cement, and did it get hot! We decided to wait 'til evening and dig it after the day cooled down.

One of these boys helping was named Ted. Ted was from the Deep South and was the most superstitious person I have ever seen. He didn't like this graveyard detail at all, but we convinced him he had nothing to worry about, so we went to digging again that evening. The moon came out as bright as the sun and we were just about done.

Now this Henry's wife had died the winter before, and we were digging his grave right next to hers. She was a huge, fat lady and they

Threshing grain.

couldn't find a coffin large enough so they built one out of two by tens. Well, as I was saying, we were just about done. Gene jumped in the grave and measured the width. Ted was down there with a pick. Gene said, "Got to dig that corner out wider." Ted said, "I'll get it," and he gave a pry and out came a piece of two by four. He said, "How'd that two by four get way down in here?" Someone said, "Oh, that's part of the old lady's casket. We must have this grave out of line." Ted flew out of that grave and took off across the field on a run. When we got home and in the bunkhouse, no Ted, and we have never seen Ted since. He didn't stop for his wagon or spare clothes. I guess his presence was demanded elsewhere.

Every rancher had four to twenty or more teams of horses. Most of them were never used except during haying. Some of these horses never worked over ten days in a year as most people would change teams at noon and drive fresh ones as often as they could. Consequently, if you wanted to see excitement, just get on a high spot and watch the meadows. I've heard people say on some of the large ranches they've seen as many as five runaways going on at the same time.

We were short one team one time and Dad saw Old Jones that lived over on the river, and borrowed a team he wasn't using. He told Dad that they'd run a bit if they got a chance. Well, I went and got the team and we put them on a dump rake. They'd run a bit alright, every time you hitched them up.

One morning a short, fat guy walked in right after breakfast

Cutting hay today.

looking for work. Dad said, "Are you a teamster?" He said, "If you can lead them, I can drive them." Well, Gene and me helped him hitch them to the dump rake and each of us was holding a horse's head waiting for him to take the seat. He said, "Wait a minute, boys," and went into the shop. When he came out, he had a piece of harness tug with a butt chain on it, climbed up on the rake, picked up his reins and said, "Turn them loose." Now, as that team left in high gear, he hollered, "Pride, Style," and came down on their butts with that butt chain. Did he rake hay? He did more raking than any two dump rakers in the country. By the end of haying, he sure had a team, but they'd forgotten this runaway stuff for sure.

A FORMAL EDUCATION

Whoa up, right here! I'm gettin' the cart before the horse. I must tell you about my formal education.

It all came about in an old country school with two old Chick Sales outhouses out behind, one marked "Girls" and one marked "Boys." They didn't give us the dignity of writing "Ladies" and "Gentlemen" on the doors. Had a Montgomery Ward catalog in each one. None of this soft stuff rolled up nice on a piece of pasteboard.

As I remember, at the start there were six pupils, two Reinoehl boys, one Praust girl, me and my two brothers. That poor girl sure caught it. We'd catch her and put a handful of grasshoppers down her neck, garter snakes in her lunch bucket, frogs in her coat pocket. Finally, she got smart and she could beat the livin' life out of any two of us, so we had to look for other entertainment.

Well, the poor school teacher was our next victim. We sure gave her a rough time. Oh, we were a real sharp, rough crew 'til the school board entered into it. When they got mixed up in this thing they called discipline, there was no contest.

Now, our first teacher was a gal, Mary McCloddy, from Butte, an Italian about six feet tall and only a few years older than us boys, fresh out of Dillon Normal School and on her first teaching job—really a wonderful gal and still enjoyed a good time. She'd go skiing with us and sleigh riding down the steepest hills, a good sport, but I guess we just took advantage of her.

In these old country schools, the teacher always boarded with some of the kids' parents. Mary lived at our place and was always pleasant company. Her and my Mom were great friends, too much so sometimes 'cause she'd tell Mom what went on in school. Then Mom couldn't keep it to herself. She'd tell Dad and the battle would start anew with us losin' real bad. The saying is that "Education is expensive." I can sure go along with that. I paid quite a bit for mine.

Mary was great on discipline. She'd get a handful of kindling and say, "You stand still." Then she'd hit us across the butt with those sticks. If you'd throw your rear end to meet that handful of kindlin', causing her to twist her hand on the sticks, she'd get a handful of slivers. We'd feel so sorry for her we'd help pull them out. She finally gave up on the handful of kindlin' and got some willow switch that had more authority, and she put on a glove. I suspect Mom gave her the idea because she knew how the willow stung.

Our Dad built us a sleigh about ten feet long. The runners were made out of two by twelves standing on edge and had a plank for a seat. The bottom of the runners had metal shoes that make it slide easy.

We had a saddle horse that could sure run—raced him anytime we saw someone who thought he had a fast horse. Old St. Elmo never lost a race that I know of. He sure could carry the mail.

Well, Gene and I hitched him to this new sled. Sure got some

Gene and St. Elmo

—40—

"uptown" rides for a while but finally he got so Gene could steer him and stop him sometimes. At least he'd stop before he went in the barn. Sometimes, if you were to ride on the back end you'd have to hold St. Elmo's head 'til everyone was seated on the sled, then as they went by, you'd jump on the back of the sleigh if you were fast enough. You learned to not miss that sled 'cause you'd walk home from school if you missed it.

Gene would set in front with his feet up against a sort of dashboard, then Lawrence right behind him with his legs around Gene, me next with my feet around Lawrence. He'd hold onto my feet, then Mary, me holding onto her long legs and she holding on to me, both arms wrapped around my waist. We were all sort of tied together that way and nobody's feet dragging in the snow.

Well, this day we all got loaded and Gene got St. Elmo down across the bridge on the creek below the school, made the turn down the flat to home. No trouble. From here it was about three-fourths of a mile and a good hard trail clear to the ranch. When we made that turn headed for home, Old St. Elmo sort of looked back over his shoulder, swinging his head from side to side and Gene hollers, "Hang on!" We knew that old pony was set for a quick trip home. That old canner took the bit in his teeth and we were underway.

Everything was going fine except mighty sudden we hit a bumpy spot, and when the sled went up and came back to the ground, Mary missed that tail board and sets on the ground. She held onto me and I held onto her feet. Did you ever hear a woodpecker on a dead tree when he's diggin' for grubs? Well, that's what Old Mary's butt sounded like bouncing on that frozen trail. Finally, she lost her hold on me. I still had her by the feet and I didn't have time to let go of her feet! She was screaming at me and bouncing along mighty fast. Gene's hollering, "Let her go. I can't stop Old Sainty." I let go of her feet and we sure flew the rest of the way. When we made that sharp turn around the house and to the barn, the sled upset. We went rolling in the snow, but we were home.

We had all our chores done and were in the house when Mary came hobbling in. If there ever was a mad schoolmarm, she was it. Blamed me for the whole shebang. I'll admit mebby I could have turned her loose sooner, but after that engagement we had with a piece of willow that day, the muscles that worked my fingers wouldn't let my fingers work. The good thing about it all was—there was no school for three days because Mary couldn't walk too well and couldn't sit either.

I suppose you wonder what we did for entertainment on those long winter evenings. We had an old radio but the batteries were always run down, no TV, telephone or electric lights—not even a phonograph.

Both Mom and Dad were great singers. Mom had a beautiful alto voice and must have known a thousand songs. She could chord accompaniment on the old pump organ and a five string banjo. Dad could really sing and when he sang tenor with Mom, you stopped and listened. We also played carrom, dominos, checkers and tiddley winks, lots of homespun games and there were a few fights. A bunch of boys need this.

Us boys started to show interest in playing that old five string banjo as we sang the songs Mom taught us, so she decided we should learn to play music, either a piano or a violin. Dad and her sure couldn't afford a piano so she got out the old Montgomery Ward catalog and sent for a beautiful fiddle.

When it arrived through the mail, it was a great day. We sat around while she tuned it up and played a few tunes. It was great. We all gave her a trial. Gene could play part of "Home Sweet Home" before we went to bed. Mom said, "You're not going to play that violin by ear. I bought the lessons and you've got to learn to read notes and do it right. Gene went to work on it, but me and Lawrence just didn't have time right then. All we could get out of it was squeaks and squawks. We all sang a lot and liked music, even the little kids.

By this time, we had a new schoolmarm. Her name was Vera Lund, a sort of deadpan gal, not near as much fun as Mary. Anyway, she said to Mom, "Can I try the violin?" Mom said, "Sure," and showed her how to tighten the bow just right and tuck the fiddle under her chin. Well, Vera got the hang of this right quick-like but when she ran that bow over those strings, she'd let it slide sideways, and such screeches you never heard come out of a fiddle. Now, Mom put up with this every night after school for a few days. Then she said, "Vera, why don't you take that up to your room so's the kids won't bother you?"

Upstairs she went, music lessons and all. In a few days she came down and wanted us all to listen while she played "Old Folks at Home." If the guy that wrote that song had a heard her, he'd have killed himself and Vera, too.

Us boys' bedroom was right next to hers. She'd practice every night. You can't imagine the moans and groans that came through those walls. It sure didn't take long to discourage us boys from learning to play that fiddle. My brother, Wendell, still has that old fiddle, but I never hear him play it and he's a real musician and sings and plays the guitar all the time.

About this time Mom started patronizing Sears, Roebuck & Co., and I'm sure that violin caused Montgomery Ward to lose a good customer.

While I'm on this education bit, I'd like to tell you about my high school education.

When going to high school, we had to drive seventy-five miles from home to Missoula in an old Model T Ford. We couldn't do it every day because the roads were all dirt roads and it sometimes took you ten hours if it rained or snowed. If it snowed very much you just didn't go.

We carried a long piece of one-inch rope at all times and a roll of wire. If we had a flat that we couldn't fix, we'd pull the tire off the wheel, wrap this rope around the rim, wiring it to the wheel and making a solid tire. If you didn't drive too fast it would last a long time.

There were no gas stations then to stop at so you did the best you could.

Oh, yes, those old Model T engines were always burning out a rod bearing. To fix that you had to pour hot babbitt into a mold and replace it. Now you couldn't do this on the road as you needed too much equipment in the operation. What we found out that worked good in a pinch was a piece of bacon rind. Every rancher cured his own hams and bacon so you always had a piece of bacon rind with you.

If you lost a bearing you'd pull the pan off the motor, wrap a piece of bacon rind around the crankshaft and screw the bearing caps back on, put the pan back on and fill it with oil and you were ready to go. This bacon rind would last a long time before the heat and wear would burn it out again.

I'll tell you the guy that invented a pig never thought of this, I'm sure.

We rented a cabin in Missoula to stay in and we batched, usually two or three of us ranch boys from Ovando. We did our own cooking and sometimes it wasn't too good.

Now the sororities at the university would have what they called Rush Week. Each sorority would put on a party trying to get new members and they always had a big feed along about midnight.

They didn't have the coolers and refrigerators we have today, so each sorority had a big screened-in porch just off the kitchen where they'd keep their cakes, pies and sandwiches to keep cool.

We would check out the dates of all these parties and us and some buddies would raid those porches along about 10:30 or 11 o'clock in the evening. Sometimes a couple of us would go around in front and start to fight, raising an awful commotion.

When all the girls rushed out to watch, the other guys would raid their groceries and head for the cabin. Finally one of the fighters would take off on a run and the others chasing him, loudly proclaiming what he'd do if he caught him.

When we'd arrive at the cabin there would be a big eating party of high school boys and girls having a free party of their own. I'm sure none of those university gals ever starved to death but we didn't either. Some of those house mothers sure could cook!

One special night we planned a raid on the "Kappa Kappa

Gamma." They really had a snooty place and crowd.

Well, anyway, this new kid wanted to go with us. We didn't want him to but he threatened to call them so we let him tag along. His name was Gritt, redheaded and short-legged, not built for speed.

We sneaked up real quiet on this place. We had our arms full when the kitchen door opened and that house mother gave the alarm. All of us dived out the door with what we had hold of and each took off in a different direction. All except this Gritt guy. He dashes back in and grabs this big five-layer cake with pink frosting and made a run across the back lawn.

Some smart guy had stretched a wire around the lawn about six inches off the ground. When Old Gritt hit that wire he was flat on his belly with his face buried in that cake.

When those girls got through with him he was pink frosting and blood from a nosebleed, all over. He hobbled into the cabin about an hour later. Those gals sure worked him over plumb good.

This, as I remember was on a Thursday night.

Now, my folks usually came to Missoula about once a month to buy groceries for the ranch. Well, when we went to school that place was a wreck. Cake pans, Jello pudding pans and pie tins all dirty—stacked wherever there was room for them.

I was the first one home from school that night and when I walked in there was Mom with all the dishes washed and stacked in a big pile. Every time she came to town she just had to clean up our cabin.

She says, "I didn't know you could cook pies and cakes. Where did you get all these nice pans?"

Well, I finally had to tell her and was she mad!

"You return all these pans and apologize and I hope they make you work it out for all the cakes you stole."

About that time in comes Dad. Boy, did he give me a going over but I could see the merriment in his eyes.

After I promised to return the pots and pans, they left for home.

Yes, I returned the pots and pans but I did it along about one o'clock in the morning and only as far as the back steps. I really couldn't apologize because nobody was awake and it wouldn't be nice to wake a house mother from a deep, comforting sleep, would it?

Now, our landlady had a lovely blonde-headed daughter that enjoyed these forays as much as I did. This landlady was grande and spent most of her time on her ranch. She owned a cow ranch at Greenough, Montana, forty miles from town.

One day in the spring she sent a letter to Patsy with some money and told her to buy a bunch of flowers and decorate the family plot in the graveyard. Well, poor Patsy spent all the money and all of a sudden she realized Memorial Day was only three days off and her mother and relations would be in town to visit the graves and no flowers.

She came to the cabin crying and wanted help. Now I couldn't see this little girl making her eyes all red with tears so I told her to come over the next night after school and I'd see if I could help her.

Next day I saw some of my buddies and talked it over with them and we decided the best we could do was to pick some wild flowers for her. Late that night we got together, she and some of her girl friends to help us.

We had an old Model T car and a pickup and a motorcycle and headed for Sacajawea Park where there were lots of flowers. Now on the way someone would spot some flowers in a yard. Right there we'd stop and pick a bouquet, be it roses, peonies, tulips or daffodils, 'til there was no place to sit in that Ford and pickup. Old Pete Tabish had a big bouquet of daffodils tied to the handlebars of his motorcycle and away we went to the graveyard. Did we decorate that family plot! You can bet we did and all the other graves too.

Next day when this gal's mother came she really patted Patsy on the back for the great job she'd done.

As they were leaving the graveyard she said "I have never seen so many flowers in the graveyard in my life. Why, someone even put flowers on the gate and along the fence."

Now if she had read the morning newspaper she'd have known. On the front page were pictures of Sacajawea Park looking like it had just had a haircut. No flowers and an article asking for help in finding the culprits.

Every once in a while someone will asks me, "If you could change your life, would you do it?"

My first reaction is, "Yes." Then I get to thinking. Knowing what I know now I'd say, "No," because if I tried some of this stuff now I'd get caught for sure.

Geese in the valley.

UNCLE WILL

We had an uncle, Will Copenhaver, who lived in Helena, Montana. He was a doctor, an ear, eye and throat specialist. He would come over every once in a while to fish, hunt or shoot ducks along the creeks and little lakes to the south of the ranch.

One fall, after he came for a hunting trip, he found all us kids sick with colds and tonsillitis. He said to my Mom and Dad, "You round up all the kids around here and have their parents bring them here and I'll set a day, bring my nurse and I'll take the tonsils and adenoids out of all these kids at one time and put an end to this. Won't cost nobody nothin'. Put a bunch of cots or beds in that big room where the fireplace is and I'll operate on the dining room table. Then we can put the kids in there 'til they recover."

Well, the day was set and everything set up with the neighbors. There was three Reinoehl boys, their sister, five of us kids and my two cousins, Hugh and Myrtle. Uncle Will and his nurse arrived the night before. Now next morning Mom, Mrs. Reinoehl, Aunt Gertrude, Uncle Will and his nurse got that country clinic going bright and early.

They'd lay us out on the table and the nurse would slap a rag with some chloroform on our nose and Uncle Will would go to work. When he was done, they'd pack us in and lay us on a cot or mattress on the floor in the big room. I wanted to watch but they had us shut in a bedroom and wouldn't let us see. When they were through with one kid they'd open the door and grab another, kinda like brandin' calves as they came down the chute. By a little after noon the first ones were coming out from under the anesthetic, some bawling and others groaning. It sure was an assembly line deal, or should I say an unassembling line?

Uncle Will had brought a whole bunch of oysters with him and he gave my mother directions on what to do. He said, "You make a big oyster stew and give those kids nothing but the stew. Don't let them eat the

Before the operation.

oysters or any solids 'til tomorrow. Then make sure to give them only soft food. They'll have a sore throat for a day or two, but they'll be alright." He probably gave her some other directions, too, but this is all I remember.

Well, Claude Reinoehl was the last one operated on so he never woke up like the rest of us. Somehow when he did he was hungry. Seems to me he was always hungry. Well, he slipped out of the big room without any of the ladies seeing him and went to the kitchen. He spotted that kettle with all those oysters in it and by the time Mom found him he'd eaten all of them. To this day I figure he owes me a oyster feed. All I got was the juice.

By the way, do you know any doctor today that would do a mass operation such as this for free? Mebby this started malpractice suits.

Along about this time Uncle Will was driving a big Franklin four-door car. It had a big eight-cylinder flathead, air cooled motor in it. All upholstery was black leather with a spare tire mounted on the rear end. Was it a beauty! The frame was hardwood, big coil springs, no noise and a very soft ride. Well, he was buying a new one and talked my folks into buying his old car. It was a real good deal, plenty of room for the whole family at one time. Uncle Will was over one day and Dad rode home with him and drove our car back that night. He was way late in the night getting home. All of us kids were sound asleep.

The next morning when we got up we ran outside to look this car over. Gene got in under the steering wheel and I was on the passenger side, enjoying the feel of everything. Dad had parked it facing a big spruce tree right in front of the house. Gene says, "I wonder what this is," grabbing ahold of a knob on the dash. It wouldn't turn so he pulled on it. Well, that old car roared into life and headed straight at that tree. Gene grabbed the steering wheel and held her steady. We hit that tree, bounced back and hit it again. That spruce tree sort of bent at the stump and finally the bumper slid up and hooked up. The hind wheels dug at the ground for a while until it killed the engine. All this time I was trying to get out but couldn't find the door latches. When she died, Gene still had good control of her head, but we were sort of high centered on that leaning tree. I guess Dad had left it in gear the night before and, when the motor started, so did we. It was Sunday morning and we got our sermon a little early. That sermon didn't take a hold on us much because we saw Mom wink at Pa and him smiling as he turned and walked away.

Another time Uncle Will took me fishing with him. We were up Monture Creek and the fishing was great. Now Uncle Will would rather flyfish than eat, but I seemed to have two hollow legs and sure was in need of refreshments. Finally he said, "Let's go get some groceries." Boy, did that sound good. I could have eaten ten peanut butter sandwiches. When we got to the car he opened the fancy lunch box, but there were no peanut butter sandwiches. He had some Velveeta cheese, soda crackers and sardines. I'd never seen such a lunch before. I'll tell you, I ate so many greasy sardines and that cheese was out of this world, with Orange Crush to wash it down. What a uptown feast! I ate all the cheese that was left and got sick on the way home, heaved all over the place. I've had a dislike for cheese and sardines ever since. Guess I just couldn't stand prosperity. Uncle Will told my folks all about it and from the laughing they did, I guess at least he enjoyed the lunch.

He gave my brother, Gene, a long octagon barreled 30/30 Marlin rifle one time. It was a beauty. The bluing job on the steel parts was sort of mottled like. When you'd look at it from one angle it would be reddish; turn it and it would be bluish and fade into greenish black. Gene really treasured this gun and could shoot it. He just didn't miss.

We were up on Iron Mountain looking for some lost sheep that dad's herder had lost and Gene had this rifle along. Well, we spotted the old ewe and her lamb off on the hillside and were trying to drive them down off the mountain to the ranch. The only way she'd go was up and away from home. We had climbed and ran and headed her so many times that we could hardly walk, we were so tired. I was plumb pooped. Finally, we had her going downhill just as nice as could be—thought we had it made when, like a whitetail deer, she turned and ran back up this steep mountain. Gene threw up the gun and said, "For two bits I'd shoot you!" And BOOM! went the old 30/30 and end over end went that old ewe. Gene was as surprised as I was. I'm sure, running through the brush, the hammer had hooked on some bush and cocked the gun without him knowing it and when he touched the trigger, that's all she wrote.

I know we ate mutton for a few days but can't remember about the lamb. Suppose we caught it and packed it home. Gene still has that rifle I'm very sure. It was a beauty, only self reliant.

When fishing was good on the North Fork.

FISHING

Fishing was us boys' thing. I believe, if we could have made a living just fishing, we'd have all been millionaires by the time we were 15 years old.

A plain hook and a worm or grasshopper was all we asked for, but if we could find two bits that would buy two Royal Coachman and a Grey Hackle, we'd believe in angels and all the other good things. All the creeks were excellent fishing and the North Fork of the Blackfoot was heaven. Cooper Lake couldn't be beat in the wintertime and Browns Lake was full of silver salmon up to two to three pounds, both summer and winter.

I remember Dad built us what he called a "skow." It was a flat bottom boat about five feet wide and fourteen feet long. It sure was our pride and joy. We'd load it on the Old Model T truck and head for Browns Lake. Five or six of us could fish at the same time. We developed a system of when you wanted to cast your line out, you'd holler, "Cast," then only cast sideways to the boat and you'd not tangle up your line with someone else's.

If we could catch the lake when a west wind was blowing, there was a cove over on the east side that would be real calm. The fish would hole up over there and, such fishing! One such evening four of us caught sixty-seven fourteen- to sixteen-inch salmon. Also, there was no limit on Silvers at that time, but there was on trout in the streams and the river. This didn't bother us much, but you always had to watch out for Old Harry Morgan, the game warden.

When haying was over, we'd go up the North Fork of the Blackfoot for a day or two. We'd camp out up by the Big Slide and Smoke's Cabin. This was always the real thing—a camp out overnight. Now someone always had to do the dishes, and I'm sure you know how boys just love to do dishes. To stop any arguments, we made a deal. The guy that caught the least number of fish on one cast had to do the dishes.

Proof of the lie.

Marg and a catch.

Sometimes we'd have five or six hooks on the same line.

Now when you'd hook a fish, you'd let him swim around 'til another one bit another fly on the same line. If you were skilled enough at keeping the right tension on your line, you could catch three or four at the same time, most of them from ten to fourteen inches long, all cutthroat, except once in awhile a small Dolly Varden. The most I ever saw was five at a time. Now, I'll tell you, that's fishing! We'd file the barbs off the hook so we could just give them some slack and they'd shake the hook.

Then there were the "bull holes." These were deep holes with big rocks for those Old Dollies (Dolly Varden) to hide under. They'd congregate in them before they went up river to spawn. We'd fish for them and catch some fifteen to twenty pounders. Usually turned them loose because we had too many fish, but it sure was a young lad's heaven anyway.

A few years ago, we took the grandkids ice fishing to a lake up in Deer Park. All these kids were real small, preschool age.

I cut a hole in the ice, and showed Todd how to fish. As he dropped his hook in the water, just as it cleared the ice, I saw this fish hit his hook. I grabbed the line and gave it a jerk, setting the hook. I hollered, "Run backwards, Todd." He sure did. As he pulled the line, the fish lined up at that hole, swimming fast. With Todd's pulling and his speed, he just flew out like a bird, landed right at Todd's feet, flopping about on the ice. Todd took one look and started across the lake to his mother screaming, "Mom, Mom, Mom!"

It took a long time to get him back to that hole and fishing again, but since that first fish, you have no problem with that now. That trout was a three and one-half pound eastern brook. It surely made fishermen and women out of his cousins. You don't have to ask them twice to go with you now.

Keeping your feet dry.

TRAPPING

When we first came to this beautiful valley it inspired us boys with a power that shaped our lives forever. We read everything we could get our hands on about hunting, fishing and trapping—*Call of the Wild* by Curwood, *Liege Mounts Free Trapper, Silver Tip, King of Grizzlies* and any stories about old mountain men, trappers and hunters. Then our valley had some well-known trappers; Kid Young, the Praust Boys and Old Joe Statler. All of these men trapped beaver, marten, fisher and bear. To say the least, they had an audience of good listeners.

Gene and I started trapping along the creeks on the ranch for mink, muskrat, weasel and badger. We had good teachers as these men I mention would show us how to set traps and skin animals and prepare the pelts for sale, how to mix up scent for use for bait, how to cover your traps and leave no human sign or smell. We really idolized these men and dreamed of the day we could put on a pair of snowshoes and head over the mountains to the Danaher or Statler Creek, even to Whiskey Ridge and Adolph's bear camp. The old Praust cabin burned in the 1988 fire on Whiskey Ridge. I have spent many a night in that cabin while trapping for marten and Canada lynx.

I remember one special time when my brother, Gene, set a trap for a badger. When he set the trap and anchored it, he allowed too much slack in his trap chain. This allowed the badger to back down his hole in the ground too far. Now a badger, if he gets back in his hole when caught in a trap, will dig the hole full of dirt and turn crossways in the hole and you cannot pull him out. Well, this is what happened this time and that night it froze hard, freezing the new dug dirt just like cement.

When Gene got to his set that night after school, this is what he found so he came home and he and I took a pick and shovel and started to dig that badger out. Well, we ended up leaving our pick and shovel there that night. Next day we went right from school and dug our hearts out. Finally, we uncovered the badger and was he a big old boy!

When we got him all skinned out and his pelt dried and ready to ship to Mass & Stefinson Fur Co. in St. Louis, Missouri, we knew we were rich cause he was the biggest badger anybody ever saw. Finally, the mail came with a big envelope and our check for the last shipment of furs. Were we excited! Listed on the price was muskrats, $.85 apiece, mink, $12.50, one hair badger, ten cents.

Now there are two different kinds of badger, a fur badger and a hair badger. A fur badger at that time would bring anywhere from $7.50 to $25.00 apiece, depending on the size. Hair badger, five to ten cents. We learned. Two nights work with a pick and shovel for ten cents! At least we had no trouble with the IRS.

We caught lots of muskrat, mink and weasel. There were a number of lakes over in the rolling hills south of home that had lots of rats. We learned to find their feed holes in the ice. We'd cut a hole big enough to set an eight by ten board in the water, put some moss on the board and apples or carrots for bait and two traps on board, then cover it over with cattail reeds and cover it with snow leaving an air space above the board. The rats would swim under the water to these places to feed and when they climbed up on the board we had them. We learned never to disturb their houses or bank dens as they'd leave and make new ones you couldn't find under the snow.

I can remember one time we got a check from Beckman Brothers Fur House in Great Falls, Montana, for $129 dollars. We were sure some of the rich people then. What did we do with all that money? Well, we sent to Monkey Wards and bought some new traps. Well, I can remember $4.25 a dozen for No. 1 Victor traps. Today, you would pay that much for one trap. Also, we bought some fishing flies. You could get three Royal Coachman or three Gray Hackle for twenty-five cents. Yes, I said three for twenty-five cents.

To me, this was the greatest education in the business world for a young lad. You learned the value of money and you did it by your own sweat. Too bad kids today can't experience it. Now, everyplace there are rats or mink, there's a "No Trespassing" sign.

One year a man by the name of Virgil Harper advertised he'd pay $30 apiece for any live mink in good health you brought him. If they had hurt their leg in a trap, no deal.

Gene and me watched our traps close and caught a big male and a large female mink. They were real dark furred, about as good as mink could be. We put them in Mom's copper wash boiler and next day hooked up a team to the sleigh and headed for Virgil's with our mink. It was about eight or ten miles to his place over southwest of Brown's Lake. Now this is in the middle of the winter and real cold. As we passed around the south end of Kleinschmidt Lake, there sat an old timber wolf on a little knob, just watched us go by, and us with no gun. Now, he'd have been worth four mink. Were we disgusted!

Late that afternoon we drove up to Virgil's house. No smoke coming out of the chimney and no dogs. Just a note on the door, "Gone to California for a couple of months." So it was take our mink home with our disappointment, skin them and ship them to some fur house and hope they thought they were as good a mink as we did.

Well, high school and making a living took over for a few years. We got into the outfitting business, guiding hunting and fishing parties. One of our guides talked me into trapping the back country in the winter with him.

We would pack our supplies into our trapping camps during the last of hunting season, cutting enough wood at each camp to last through the winter and winterizing each camp so we'd be cozy warm and dry in any kind of weather.

Our first camp was at Lake Otatsy at 7,000 feet, eighteen miles from the ranch. The next was on Dwight Creek, another fifteen miles north, then the Old Danaher Cabin at Danaher, twelve miles farther on.

We would then run our traplines back south to the Praust Cabin on Whiskey Ridge twelve miles from here. Then, we'd climb back up Canyon Creek to Lake Otatsy Cabin, making a big circle, each of us setting traps through a different part of the country, but ending up at these given camps at night.

Our main game was marten (Russian Sable) and Canada Lynx. We would each have around 500 traps set out so it kept you busy each day checking your traps in different areas. You could check each trap for a week sometimes and not catch a thing. Then the weather would change and all the animals would be on the move it seemed, and you'd really be busy skinning and stretching fur for a few days. You always had to check those traps regular or you would lose fur to other animals and hawks and owls. The anticipation you experienced every morning when you strapped on your snowshoes and hit the trail was unbelievable.

I always said the richest I have ever been was when I topped a high ridge, and as far as I could see, I owned the whole country. Not another human track in the snow, not a sound except the crash of silence and the beauty of nature, green and white with such a blue sky. If you'd have ever seen this as I have, you would never wonder how they call Montana "The Big Sky Country."

There were also times when you longed for Florida or sunny Arizona. One time Bill and I were going to check some new country for marten. We planned on a twenty-mile circle as the weather was beautiful and the snowshoeing good. We started out early and planned to be back at Lake Otatsy that night.

Along in the afternoon, the clouds started to build in the northeast and the wind got gusty. We were on top of Lake Mountain just under the Lookout cabin when this Northeaster hit us. The wind was so strong we couldn't stand up and it would suck all the air out of your lungs. We took our coats off and wrapped them around our heads and crawled up the mountain to the fire lookout cabin. The temperature must have been 25 degrees below zero.

We didn't think we'd ever make it as there was no trees for protection. We just went on our hands and knees leaning against each other. When we got to the cabin there was a lock on the door. Old Bill says, "I got a key," and pulled his six shooter out and unlocked that door.

There was lots of wood in the cabin and stacked along the outside. We got a fire going in the stove. You couldn't warm that shack up no way. We left the oven door open and shoved wood in that stove for three nights and two days.

All we could find to eat in there was some canned brown bread, a little cheese and tea. We'd melt snow for water but before you could get the tea made, the water was cold. I'll tell you that was the coldest hotel I ever spent time in and the food service was sure rotten.

The third morning broke out clear but awful cold. By daylight we had our snowshoes on and headed for our camp at Lake Otatsy. That place looked like the Waldorf Astoria when we came out of the heavy timber across the lake. It didn't take us long to have two stoves going and food in a skillet and coffee in the pot. I'll tell you, we really enjoyed a couple of coffee royals before supper was done and let the traps take care of themselves the next day.

About this time, there were a lot of silver fox farms in Montana and Canada that raised silver fox for fur. They wanted to start raising marten in captivity so were offering $50 apiece for live marten. Bill and I would catch them alive and put a collar on them and keep them in the cabin 'til we got four or six of them, then one of us would pack them out to the ranch on a packboard that we'd made a wire basket for.

While at the cabin, we fed the marten dried prunes and figs. They sure liked them and some of them got so tame you could turn them loose in the cabin. They'd run around the cabin like a kitten. We'd roll a prune across the floor and they'd chase it like a house cat, catch it and run for their little house, go inside, eat it and go back to sleep.

The fur farmer never did figure out how to raise marten. They would breed in captivity but when the female had her young, she would kill all of them. There must have been something lacking in their diet that they got while in the wild but was not duplicated in captivity.

These winters in the hills trapping gave me the opportunity to study and watch different animals, learn their habits and how they survived. One animal I watched was the River Otter playing and fishing. I lay on the bank in the tall grass and watched two of them one time on the Danaher Creek fishing. I always imagined they just dove into the water and outswam the trout when they caught them. Well, that's not how they did it at all.

There was a deep hole in this river so clear you could see the fish feeding just below where the swift water ran into this big pool. Mr. Otter would run up river along the bank. When he got up along the rapids, he would swim out in the middle of the current and sink to the bottom like a rock. Now the current would roll them along the bottom like a water-soaked stick. When the otter was under the feeding fish, he would come alive like a flash and catch a fish, come to the surface and swim to shore and have lunch, then do it again. I have seen piles of fish on the bank of 10 or 12 good sized trout with only a bite out of their back. I'm sure it was the otter's way of having a good time as well as dinner.

I watched the elk play. Sometimes they would run in a big circle like as if they were playing tag or some other game. Then you'd see two of them stand on their hind legs facing each other and look as if they were boxing. Other times they'd put their front feet around each other's neck and hop around and around like some kind of dance.

The coyotes would run in packs in the Danaher Valley and pull down many elk each winter. When the elk spotted a lone coyote crossing

Mountain country.

the meadows they would line up with a bunch of cows in front in a solid line, the calves and young stuff right behind them. These old cows would kinda run on their hind legs while pawing with their front feet and go after that coyote. I'll tell you, that coyote would sure head for the first timber he saw and didn't come back for more. You let that same coyote and a couple of his buddies catch one of those cows out on the flat by themselves at night and they'd have elk steak for a few days.

When we were at Danaher Cabin, we'd hear the coyotes running elk at night. When they made a kill, they would eat 'til they were full, then set down and howl at the stars. Sometimes it would sound like there was 20 of them howling at the same time. We'd go outside and listen to locate where they were at. The next morning one of us would take some traps, we usually used three No. 3 traps, and a roll of wire and go find the kill. If the coyotes had not opened up the body cavity, we'd dress that elk, rolling the entrails out to the side. Then we'd set three traps in the chest cavity, tying two of them up next to the front by the throat area and another just inside the rib cage. We'd take long pieces of wire, fasten them to the trap chain and to the elk's leg, and go away and leave it. If the weather was cold, our scent would freeze and dissipate in a couple of nights and the outside of the elk would freeze like cement.

Now when the coyotes came to feed, they would crawl into the chest cavity to eat and we'd have a coyote. When the trap snapped on his foot, he'd take off on a run out to the end of the wire, find he couldn't get loose and lay down in the snow. Along would come his buddy and do the same thing. Next morning you'd have a couple of coyotes. I've got as many as three coyotes on one elk in one night. Their pelts were worth from $10 to $15 apiece so it paid off.

A lot of these coyotes were hybrids crossed with the Grey Timber Wolf. Their pelts were light in color with a blue under fur and extremely large. The average coyote has a brownish cast to the color of his fur so the hybrids brought the most money.

One of the animals I really enjoyed trapping was the fox. He is so smart that he really taxes your ability. With a coyote or lynx you make your set so they have to come in the front to get the bait. Now a fox will most generally sneak up behind and come in the back door, so's to speak.

My best luck was to place my bait on a tree, then build a covey or a shelter over the bait, branches covering it so's you can see it only from the front. Now a fox would sneak up behind the tree and reach around and steal the bait without disturbing your set. I'd build a covey, place my bait in the front, then place a trap up close to the tree on the back side. Mr. Fox would sneak around behind the tree and reach for the bait and step in the trap. All the time he thought the trap was in front under the bait.

Another was to dry a rabbit skin and cut it into a ten-inch square, then use a piece of thread tied to the corner, and hang it on a limb about five feet from the ground and place a trap under it. The natural breeze will keep the rabbit skin twisting and turning in the air. A fox sees this and he keeps walking around it in circles ending up right under it looking up at it and steps in your trap.

While we were tending our traps, I would take one side of the valley and Bill the other. He'd have his traps along the mountains on one side and I on the other. That way, each night we'd end up at the same camp. The next day we'd go on to the next camp.

One day in March, it was awful warm and I was on the sunny side of the valley and the snow got so soft and sticky I couldn't keep it from balling up on my snowshoes. I was only about four miles from camp so I crossed the river and climbed up to Bill's snowshoe trail where the snow was still frozen and not so sticky. His snowshoe trail came to a deep ravine where a little creek came down the mountain. There were two big logs laying parallel across the ravine covered heavy with snow. To keep from climbing down and out of that steep gulch, Bill had made his trail across those logs on top of about four feet of snow. This saved a lot of hard climbing and we did it a lot.

Well, this day the snow had softened up and as Bill crossed the logs the snow gave away and Bill fell down between the logs, but his snowshoes hooked up on the logs. When I came in sight, there was Bill hanging head down and black in the face. He could not reach the harness on his feet to loosen himself to get out of this jam. I crawled out there and cut his feet loose from the snowshoes and Bill fell to the snow below. He said he'd been there a long time and was so tired of trying to get loose he just couldn't lift his body up anymore. If I hadn't come along right then, Bill would have died. A man can only hang head down a short time.

It sure taught Old Bill and me not to take such chances. A guy don't have to spend much time in the bush to learn to be real cautious because you're a long way from help and all alone, generally.

The last winter I trapped was the winter of 1939 and '40. It was a very profitable year for Bill and I. We got a lot of marten and lynx and muskrats. We topped the Seattle Fur Exchange with our fur with an average of $30 per pelt.

The next fall I joined the Navy and by the time the War No. II was over Marg and I were married and I've been trying to make a living ever since.

Every young man ought to have such an experience in his lifetime.

The Old Lady.

MRS. LAWRENCE

In the early days of Ovando and Helmville, everything was freighted in by wagon teams from either Missoula or Drummond, groceries, hardware, clothes, anything sold by the local merchants at their stores. Among these freighters came Mrs. Lawrence and her husband Bill from down Salt Lake way.

Mrs. Lawrence was a big woman, over six feet, and I would guess her as well over 200 pounds, no fat, just big and rough. She'd walk into the saloons, put her foot on the rail and drink with any cowboy, freighter or rancher and never show a sign of the booze bothering her. She always wore a long dress of dark material, clear, to her ankles. She was a big, rough Danish woman with a booming voice and a heart as big as the great outdoors. If someone was sick or needed help, Mrs. Lawrence's team was tied up at their gate before anyone else ever knew of the people's problems. I can remember my folks talking and wondering how she always was the first to get there.

Her husband, Bill, homesteaded on a piece of ground east of Ovando on the bank of the North Fork of the Blackfoot River when freighting kind of petered out due to new ways of transportation to the valley. Bill was a little guy and a cook. He didn't like work too well, so Mrs. Lawrence did it all.

After Bill died, she got a few milk cows, sold the cream, raised a few calves, pigs and chickens to get along. Finally, she either sold or lost the homestead (I never knew) and rented the Old Lund ranch up on Kleinschmidt Flat. This ranch was surrounded by land owned and leased by two cow outfits from over south of the Big Blackfoot River. They did not believe in fixing fence or care whose ground their cattle were grazing on as long as it was their cattle doing the grazing.

By this time, the Old Lady (her common name) had fifteen or twenty head of half milk cows and Hereford cross that produced lots of

Mrs. Lawrence's home.

milk. She couldn't milk them all so she figured a way to make a good living for her and her dogs. She had dogs of every kind, one St. Bernard, five or six mongrels and some sort of a poodle, a little bit of a feisty thing.

When calving time came along she'd take her team and old buckboard and go for a ride out on the Flat and highgrade any newborn calf she could catch. If this calf outran her, she'd say, "Pike, you catch him." Pike was the big St. Bernard dog. He'd get that calf and lay on him 'til the Old Lady come to put him in the buckboard. Then she'd take the calves home and put them to nursing the milk cows. After a day or two the cows didn't care how many calves sucked as long as they sucked. I saw as many as four calves following one old milk cow. I also remember the Old Lady Lawrence saying, "Them guys don't know nothin' about the cow business. Just look at the dry cows they've got and all of my cows have twins or triplets."

She would fight like a man and always had this old, long Tom shotgun under the seat. I don't believe she'd ever use it, but I'm sure the guys that owned the cattle believed otherwise. One day in the 30's this rancher caught her out in his field with the buckboard and a calf or two. He was driving a Model A Ford car. When he was giving her hell about stealing his calves, she grabbed him, stuck his head through the window of the car, then cranked the window up, almost choking him, got in her buckboard and went home. Two of this old boy's men found him late that night, almost choked to death and half frozen. He never bothered the Old Lady again.

About this time the bank foreclosed and sold her cattle, and she

She was successful.

lived in a cabin on the ranch. We bought the ranch and Mrs. Lawrence died a year after, right in the cabin in her sleep.

We all have our shortcomings, but I can say no one ever went by Mrs. Lawrence's that wasn't invited in, fed and offered a bed if needed, nor did she ever not help anyone in need. I'm sure anyone who knew her would say the same thing. She was big, rough, tough, but she could not hide that beautiful, big heart.

It must have been along in 1933 or 1934 that my brother, Lawrence, and I drove up to the Old Lady's place, left our Ford in the yard and went up the mountain hunting. We were looking for some of those mossy horned mule deer that hung out high on the Cooper Lake Range. Iron Mountain was our destination. We'd seen some big heads up there in the summer and knew right where to go.

Now, back then it was rare to see an elk in this country. There were a few in Spring Creek and on the head of Monture Creek, but you had to go over into Meadow Creek or up the North Fork and into the Danaher country to get any good elk hunting. In our search for those trophy bucks, Lawrence and I got separated.

After hunting hard I sat down on a log beside a creek and was eating a sandwich. All of a sudden I heard some noise coming down the creek. I figured it was Lawrence so just sat there with my rifle leaning against a tree about ten feet from me. I was about to whistle to let him know where I was, when out of the brush walks this cow and calf elk. Was I surprised! Right behind them came some more. I counted eleven head before I made a dash for my rifle. Those elk made a dash, too, right into a thicket. I was bemoaning my luck, or stupidity, when out walks this raghorned bull. He looked like an elephant for size to me. He just stood there looking after his cows. I finally came awake, grabbed my rifle and let go. He ran into the timber and I ran after him, ignorant about following wounded game. My shot was clean and he lay right at the edge of the trees.

I dressed him out and headed down the mountain for Mrs. Lawrence's house and help. When I got to her house she really ribbed me because there was no elk on that mountain. I was just a dumb kid who didn't know the difference between an elk and one of those stinky old mule bucks. I asked if I could borrow a couple of horses to pack him down off the mountain. She said, "Hell, no. I'll get two saddle horses and go with you. You probably couldn't find him. Anyway, if it's an elk, you couldn't lift them quarters up on a horse." So away we went. I knew where I was going and when we rode up to the elk, all she could say was, "Lawdy! Lawdy! Land of Blessed Saints. It is a bull elk. Guess you know what you're doin' kid."

We quartered the elk and, by this time, Lawrence showed up and he'd got a big buck. We loaded the horses and walked off that mountain. I felt like a king or something to have her say I was all right. Since that time, the elk have increased and many elk have been taken off of those mountains. Many of my first lessons in hunting game was gained hunting those same mountains.

Cooper Lake lay to the north of her place about a mile following the creek from the house. The best cutthroat trout fishing I've ever experienced was through the ice in this lake. In the wintertime we'd go up to her place by team and sleigh, stay all night with her, and the next morning put on snowshoes and hike up to the lake and fish through the ice. Most of the fish were fourteen to eighteen inches long and weighed a pound up to two and one-half pounds. Beautiful red-bellies we called them. There was usually our Dad and Ezra Reinoehl and all us boys there from each family.

Now Mrs. Lawrence's house was a big, old log house built in 1886. The upstairs was not finished, just inch boards for a floor and a couple of iron beds up there with old, saggy mattresses and springs. After a spuds, meat and gravy supper, she'd say, "All you youngins up that stairs and get to bed. You're going to need it if you make the lake tomorrow." The six of us kids would finally get our beds made and have several wrestling matches in between.

When she had breakfast ready we'd be dead to the world. She'd call breakfast once. If no one showed up sudden like, she'd open the stair door and say, "Pike, go get them." You did not sleep any more cause Pike and all the other dogs would be up that stairs and you sure got dressed and down to breakfast or those dogs would drag you down the stairs without any clothes. I'll tell you, us boys loved that Old Lady. She was the biggest doll I ever knew.

One day a group of fishermen came out of the hills from the Danaher where they'd been on a two week fishing trip. As they were unloading their pack horses, Old Pike, the St. Bernard dog, got in the way. This big, young man over six-foot tall says, "Get out of here," and he kicked Old Pike in the butt. The next thing he knew he was laying on the ground and Mrs. Lawrence was kicking him in the belly saying, "You son of a _____. I'll teach you to kick my little dog."

Most of these old-timers are gone now, and there are few who remember them. I hope my brother has a picture of her so I can put it with this little yarn.

Mrs. Lawrence had a brother from down Salt Lake, Denver and California way. She never knew where he was until he showed up at her place. She called him "Sir Andrew" or the "Duke." I'm sure he never worked an hour in his life and sure didn't plan on it.

He always drove a good car and seemed to have plenty of money. He was a very striking-looking man, tall, slim and very well met, appeared to have a good education, claimed to have gone to Brigham Young University. When asked what he did for a living, he claimed he was a professional entertainer, and I'm sure he was.

Well, he showed up one year and had this young guy with him. Howard was his first name. Said he was his chauffeur. Howard was a big Danish kid that showed a lot more manual labor than a chauffeur should have shown. When Sir Andrew got ready to go back to Salt Lake or Denver or wherever, Howard said, "I'm staying here. I like this country."

Anyway, we hired Howard. He was a hard worker and a good hand. We boys and he got to be good friends, so he got to telling about his chauffeur job and Sir Andrew. Now, Sir Andrew never stayed too long in one spot, he kept on the move. It seems he would drive into Denver, St. Louis, or Frisco and get ahold of the social calendar and find out where all the big wealthy parties were at and time and dates. Then he'd fix himself up a party calendar to plan his goin's on. He'd get himself all shined up in a tux, top hat and coat, have Howard drive him by this party place real slow. He'd step out and walk around a Cadillac or limo like he'd just got out of it. Then up the walkway to the door and on in and crash this party. If there was a doorman, he'd greet him with so much friendliness that the doorman just had to recognize him or be embarrassed because he didn't know these people's friends. I'm sure he made a very striking figure when all dressed up, and as far as conversation, he'd surely not lack that.

Seemed like, when the party got going good, Sir Andrew would

Sir Andrew the Duke.

raid that place for jewels, cash or anything he could put in his pocket, thank the hostess and proclaim his sadness at having to leave early, step out and join whoever was waiting for him around the block. By daylight they'd be well on their way for parts unknown.

It was a little risky, but beat working, so Sir Andrew told him. Howard figured common labor sure would beat hard labor over a rock pile with a sledge.

GEORGE, HORSES

All my life I've been a guy who was deeply interested in the past. At least I guess that is the way to say it. Whatever other people have done is of great interest to me. I can listen intently to old people, especially those that have early-day experiences. Good or bad they stick with me. Many of the old-timers of this country had such rare experiences on both sides of the law, making each a way of life in its own realm. One such story I'd like to tell you about involves two old friends. I was a kid and they were men way up in years. At least they were "smooth mouthed." In horse talk this means old and over the hill.

They had been horse thieves in their younger years but respected ranchers at this time. I was a slick-eared kid with lots of questions and plenty of time to listen. They loved to talk and show me some of the old tricks of the trade, how to rope a horse and how to run a brand on a stolen horse so it looked old. Then Old George told me how he and Hubert met the first time and became partners 'til death broke up their friendship. Both are dead and gone years ago.

Hubert was by far the best hand I ever saw with a ketch rope. My friends, Trixi McCormick, Monty Montana, Eddy Carol and others could do more tricks spinning ropes and making fancy catches of several horses at a time, all great entertainment, but out on the hills and in the brush Old Hubert could really handle that loop—make it seem to come alive in his hands.

He'd make a big loop in his rope and lay it on the ground, twist it into a figure eight, then pick it up, having two loops in one hand. Then he'd say, "Kid, run that horse by me." As the horse came running down the corral fence he'd give a flip of his wrist and that loop would snake out in front of that horse's front feet, each end of the loop picking up a different foot. He set back on the rope and the horse would fall. Now as the horse went down, he'd flip that rope up between the hind legs, then as the horse fell he'd run up to the front feet, flip the rope between the front legs, give a big jerk and the hind foot would slide up between the front feet. Next he'd take a couple of wraps around all three feet and there lay that horse with three feet tied together. He could rope and hogtie two or three in less time than I can tell you about it.

He'd make a small loop about two feet across for a head catch. He'd say, "Which horse do you want?" I'd answer, and with a flip of the wrist that little loop would sail across the corral over the other horses and settle neatly over this horse's head. Naturally, the horse would start to run on the rope and as he cleared the other horses Hubert would give the rope a jerk, straightening out the horse's neck, then a flip of his wrist and he'd have another loop on the horse's muzzle forming a neat halter on the horse's head. If the horse ran on the rope he could jerk him around to face the roper at all times.

I practiced this 'til I wore out my arms, but it was a rare accident when I got the loop on the horse's nose. One day I asked him, "How did you learn to throw such a small loop so flat just above a horse's head?" Here's what he told me. "When I was young we used to borrow any good horse we could and sometimes you'd run them into an old straw shed. Most ranchers in Montana and Canada east of the mountains had straw sheds for stock to get in to fight flies and weather out a storm in the winter. These consisted of a bunch of posts about ten feet tall set in the ground in a big square shape with woven wire stretched over the top and around the sides leaving an opening on one side so stock could come and go. Then in harvest time they would pull the threshing machine up close and as they threshed the grain they'd blow the straw in a big pile over the top of the shed making a regular straw barn so's to speak.

"Now when the horses were inside of this, you'd only have 18 inches to two feet above the horse's head so to catch one you had to keep your loop flat until it was over the horse's head. Then a slight jerk on the rope and the loop would settle down over the horse's head without disturbing the others and you could lead him out and be on your way."

He must have done lots of roping this way because he didn't miss.

One day I asked George how he and Hubert had become acquainted and he told me this story. He and another guy had picked up a few horses up in Saskatchewan and were headed south to the logging country in Idaho to sell them as they were all big draft colts and they had picked up some more as they headed for the U.S. Border.

Well, it seemed the Canadian Mounties were giving them a pretty close run so they had to travel west and south mighty fast. When they crossed the border just north of Havre, Montana, they swung west up the Milk River. These draft horses were tired and wanted to go home and they were having a hard time keeping them going and bunched. When they figured they'd lost the Mounties they slowed up and were resting the horses and themselves, camped alongside the Milk River in a big clay banked coulee. Every evening they'd see this lone rider peeping over the hill watching them. One morning as they were having coffee, getting ready to move again, this stranger rode into camp. They asked him to sit and have a cup of coffee. He said, "I been watching you boys and looks to me you could use another hand holding those broncs together. Besides, I'm headed the same direction as you are." George said, "Where's your camp?" He said, "I've got ten head in a draw west a few miles. We could throw together and I, for one, could use some help changing brands."

"Well, you've seen him rope and we sure was having trouble—too many horses for two guys. So we struck up a deal and have been together ever since."

Another thing he told me about was how they would alter brands. When you sold a horse you'd better have your brand on him or a bill of sale proving your ownership of that critter or you might be a candidate for a necktie party. Some people would brand them and hide them out someplace 'til the brand healed. Others would use a wet gunnysack and a hot iron. This method was not too satisfactory because you could easily scald a big patch on the skin and ruin the brand.

To do this, you'd wet the sack and lay it over the spot where you wanted the brand then put a white-hot branding iron on top of the sack in a quick motion, steaming the imprint of the iron on the horse's skin causing the skin to rise up, leaving a raised imprint but not burning the skin and hair all off. The brand, though fresh, would appear to be old. It would not last long but give you time to get the horses out of their home range where you could take your time and brand them right. Now this had its disadvantages, too, because you had to have a fire for a long time and the smoke was a dead giveaway as to your location. Every cowboy or rider of the open range watched for smoke from a fire. You didn't need any visitors if you were altering brands because he might own that horse you had hogtied on the ground close to the fire.

When these old boys wanted to brand some horses they would find a draw with a spring or creek in it and some hawberries or thorn bushes growing along the banks. Thorn bushes is a type of northern hardwood and real tough. They'd cut a bunch of sticks about the size of a lead pencil and sharpen one end to a needle point, then burn it just enough to harden the point, then shape it again to a very sharp point. With the blackened end they would draw a picture of the brand on the animal. Some of these guys should have been artists. With the sharpened end they would prick the roots of each hair, following the picture of the brand until each hair showed a little drop of blood, wash off the black from the burnt stick and turn the horse loose.

In three or four hours this pricked line would start to swell and you'd have an old-looking brand with the hair grown over it. It would last for three to four weeks before all the swelling went down and the outline of a brand disappeared—no raw spots or scars from the burn of a hot iron. The only way you could tell the difference in an old brand was to kill the horse and skin him. With a burned brand it would show on the flesh side of the skin.

You could move a bunch of horses a long ways in three weeks at that time, no fences and plenty of space where no people lived. I'll tell you these old boys had it down pat.

I broke saddle horses about this time and George wanted me to ride out some colts he had. So one day I went down to get them and while there I got him to show me how this branding worked. We laid my saddle horse down and right below our brand, a HEART BAR on the right shoulder we traced a new brand using this thornbush method. By the time I got home that night I had a saddle horse branded and you could hardly tell the new brand from the old one. I was riding our stallion, a Morgan, and Dad was mad as a wet hen when he saw the two brands. It was all gone in a couple of weeks so all's well that ends well! Old George says, "You'd a made a good horse thief. Mebby its a good thing I was born so cockeyed late in the settling of the Old West.

The last story I can remember George telling me was probably the last time I saw him. He went over the hill not too long after that. This happened way back in the later 1800's sometime, near Medora, North Dakota, in the Missouri Badlands. It seemed there was an old man in his nineties who had a small horse ranch right down on the river bank where there was some nice meadow grassland. He raised some fine thoroughbred horses and lived all by himself. I'll tell this as near as I can in George's words:

"Well, me and my partner had passed there several different trips when we were moving horses from Canada south and admired his stock from afar across the river. We couldn't understand the old geezer having that many good horses when he could only ride one at a time and he never sold any of them, just let them run in the breaks. We decided we should borrow some and they'd sure bring a better price than those we'd been selling down south. Well, we set up a camp and watched with a spyglass from across the river. We were well hid in the river breaks and no one knew we were in the country. We were waiting for him to go to Medora for supplies. It would take him two days and we'd figure to be long gone with some of that stock before he got home and checked it out.

"We were about out of grub, as we'd been sitting here for ten or twelve days and our feet were getting itchy. My partner said, 'Let's give him one more day. He's got to go to town pretty soon.' Then a voice right behind us and above said, 'Well, if you guys could do with some coffee let's ride over to my place and I'll scare up some coffee and the fixins'.' Sittin' on a rock up behind us with an old buffalo gun across his knees is this old man who owns the horses. Nothing else to do but accept his invite at a time like this so we get our horses and ride down across the river to his shack. All the time we're visitin' like old friends and not a word about them horses.

"He got some coffee goin' and a bite of chow. After we'd eat he said, 'I've been watching you boys since the first night you rode in and I know what you want but I'd like to tell you a story.' We rolled a Bull Durham cigarette and with a fresh cup of coffee we sat polite like. 'Years ago I lost my brother and my son at San Juan Hill and that did my wife in, so it's just me and them thoroughbred horses. Let's go look at them. I know ifn' you boys wants them that bad you can have them 'cause I can't do much about it now.' Well, we went and had a look. He had six registered mares and a stud horse that was out of this world and a bunch of their colts. Such horses! All 16 hands and muscled where they should be, a horseman's dream of real horse flesh. If he'd have given them to us we couldn't have taken them. We stayed on with him a couple of days and became such good friends that we always stopped at his place whenever we were in the Medora country. Never knew what happened to him or his horses, as I moved to Canada about that time."

I have always wondered how much truth was in these stories but I'm sure they were at least 90 percent true, for neither of them had anything to gain by telling me lies.

This had to be in 1932 because Dad had just bought a brand new Model A Ford truck from H.O. Bell in Missoula. It was a beautiful thing, roll-up windows and good heater and big one and one-half ton rig. Old George propositioned him one day to haul a ton of alfalfa seed for him from Saco, Montana, back to Ovando so they took off after the seed.

Well, now George sported a big handlebar mustache and chewed cut plug tobacco. He'd cut off a big chunk and cram it in his mouth with juice dripping off the ends of that mustache and when he spit it sure made a wet spot in the road. Riding for three or four days in that new truck cab, he'd roll the window down and sort of aim at the outside, sometimes spit before he got the window open. You should have seen the inside of that cab and the outside too. Tobacco juice everywhere and by this time, dry and hard.

Well, next day Dad and Mom were going to Missoula. When she started to get in that truck and saw all the good old juice over everything she was fit to be tied and wouldn't get in 'til Dad had washed that truck inside and out. While he was busy with his scrub job and a bucket of hot soapy water, I came by and asked, "Having some trouble?" Now, I could write down his answer but someone might have me arrested for some kind of pornography.

Howie Fly with a loaded string.

PARTIES

In this good old U.S.A., one tradition that has carried through since the Pilgrims ran into that old Plymouth Rock, has been entertainment. It is what has kept a smile on our faces and joy in our hearts. Even in the most trying of times, we've stopped for it. While the big guns were blasting and the bombs bursting, we stopped for Bob Hope and his crew of entertainers to lift our cares and cheer our hearts in World War II.

Way back as far as I can remember, it was always homespun country fun that was looked forward to above most other things; house parties, card parties or get togethers with dancing and singing, no boob tubes to glue you to the front room until your eyes burned.

Mebby I miss the feeds that all the ladies brought to any party. They always done themselves proud. What cakes and pies! All through the winter months we used to have these parties. If no one put one on, we'd just call a surprise party on some ranch family. Sometimes we'd sure catch them with "their pants down" as the old saying goes.

I remember one night when everyone dropped into this ranch, we found it was bath night. When the first ones to crash the kitchen door found the kids taking baths in the old round washtubs on the kitchen floor, there sure was a scramble for the nearest bedroom and the kids yelling for clothes. If you caught people that way today, I'm afraid there would be some noses bent, but back then it was part of the fun.

I know I've gotten to where it seems like an effort to start up the car to go someplace after supper. We used to harness four head of horses, hook them on a sleigh and drive ten or fifteen miles, dance all night and get home by daylight next morning and have one foot-shufflin' good time. During Christmas and New Year's holidays, we would have a party every other night or so. We'd feed all the sheep and cattle, then load up loads of hay for the next day so after the party all we had to do was pitch the hay to the stock and go to bed and sleep.

We'd hook up four head of horses to a big feed sleigh. The hay rack was ten feet by twenty long. We'd put about two foot of hay in it, stretch a canvas over the hay and another to cover the people, and away we'd go. We also had several kerosene lanterns that we'd light and put between the covers to keep everybody warm.

One night we were going to have a big load, so I stopped at Joe Murphy's and Jess Calvender brought out a swing team, and now we had six horses on that sleigh. From here we went to Ovando, then to the Colby and Dixon ranches, picking up people who wanted to go to the party. Then up Warren Creek to McNally's, Brunette's and Pete Jacobsen's. I guess we ended up with twenty-five or thirty people, plus all the cakes, sandwiches and pies for midnight supper.

Jess and I were standing up in the front of the rack and I was driving. They stacked all these pies, cakes, etc., in boxes right behind us giving room for everyone to sit behind this. Now, we had a long hill to go down with an S turn at the bottom. On the last turn before the road straightened out there was a big rock right alongside the road. We always ran that hill, letting the horses trot and lope down it. By the time we hit the bottom, they'd be running pretty fast to keep out of the sleigh's way.

I forgot to say before that Jess had a little jug and he and I were sampling it as we went along. When we got near the bottom of the hill, I

Those old get-togethers.

says, "Jess, I've got too many lines. Here, you take half of them." He grabbed a handful and when we came to that S turn, I hollered, "Pull those leaders wide so's we'll miss that rock. Jess pulled and threw that lead team right over that rock. When the sleigh hit that rock, it stopped right now. Away went our team with the tongue and part of the front runners, down the road. Jess had grabbed the wrong lines and turned them the wrong way.

All the pies, cakes, sandwiches and people were piled up against us and the front end of the rack. By now we had a bunch of mad women and squallin' kids and a few men who couldn't appreciate our good spirits. Down the road went our six horses, dragging the tongue and part of the sleigh. Old Lady Luck was with us. My uncle and Virgil Harper were driving a car to the party. They stopped the team and drove it back to us. Everyone was in a better mood when they saw the team coming. We got some barbed wire off Jacobsen's fence and wired our outfit together and took off to the dance again.

That night we were surprising the Reinoehl family up on Kleinschmidt Flat, about fifteen miles away. The party was going good when we arrived. If I remember, there were fifty-two men, women and kids crammed into that big log house. We danced, played pinochle and a little poker 'til daylight was breaking. Old Ezra suggested we stay for breakfast. We sure did. The women had hotcakes, bacon and eggs with coffee. What a party!

When we hitched the teams to head home, someone looked at the thermometer and it was 25 degrees below zero. Gene, Jess and I took turns driving home, changing off running behind the sleigh to keep warm. All the rest of those jokers were asleep under the top cover with the lanterns keeping them toasty. They sympathized with Gene but laughed at me and Jess.

There were two big women always at these parties, Mrs. Reinoehl and Mrs. Kuster. They were so jolly and full of fun. When it came to dancing, they were just like a feather on the floor. Mrs. Reinoehl taught me to dance. What a dancer she was! I'll never forget her. She could dance any dance ever invented. She made you feel like you had invented dancing.

All the small kids and babies were laid out crosswise on a bed someplace and slept right through the party. Claude and I would slip in there and switch clothes with some of those kids. Then when the people were getting ready to go home, you should have seen the mad scramble to make sure they had the right kid. I never saw anyone get mad about anything, they just enjoyed a good time even at their own expense.

Oh, yes, this Mrs. Kuster had a daughter that kind of took my eye at that time. When I would get her to eat supper with, that old girl would come over and sit right between us. One night, as she was taking a bite of three layer cake with lots of marshmallow frosting on it, I hit her elbow. She rubbed that frosting from her chin up into her hair. Me and that gal broke up right after that, by request.

There were always several people around that were very musical. They could play a piano, violin, banjo, squeeze box or guitar and I mean make real music. Most of them didn't know one note from the other, but really had an ear for music.

I remember one guy from Alabama who could make a violin really talk. He would start playing with a smile on his face. He also sang as he played. It always seemed the longer he played the sadder he got and the better the music got. I've seen him sitting there playing that old fiddle and singing all by himself and crying, the tears rolling down his cheeks, after most people had gone home. All of us young guys sure learned a lot of old songs from this guy. I have often wished I could have captured some of that music on a tape. There were no tape recorders at that time.

He must have had a bad hand dealt him somewhere along the line of life to cause him to get the blues every time he played that fiddle. He could really make that fiddle bring out just how he felt, happy or blue. We boys and my sister learned his style and we have enjoyed it all our lives. If you don't think so, just get Wendell to play and sing the song, "Old Shep", about a dog and a boy.

BREAKING HORSES TO RIDE

My brother, Gene, and I used to break saddle horses for people to ride. We would ride the buck out of them and have them bridle wise. Not well reined, just enough so's you could steer them and they had a healthy respect for both rider and the bit. They called it "green broke." Usually, we rode them for thirty days and received $10 a head. Now trainers get $375 to $400 for thirty days. That probably would have been too much money back then. I never had $300 in one bunch in all those years. Why, you could have bought a pretty fine car for that kind of money.

People would bring us a bronc or mebby several head of colts at a time and we would ride them out in the evenings after work and weekends.

One time we had six or seven of them in the barn and Dad needed a saddle horse. Well, he came out of the barn mad as a wet hen and says, "Where's there a gentle horse? All I can find is a bunch of knotheaded cayuses." I said, "Take that pinto stud in the corral. He's dog gentle."

Now the stud was as gentle as a milk cow. The only thing I didn't tell the Old Man was that he was whip broke. Now a horse that is whip broke is trained by using a whip so's all you have to do is wave your arm and he'll run right up to you, and you can put your bridle or hackamore on him while he just stands there. No chasing him around the corral to catch him. This is an excellent way to break a stud horse. Now this old pony was really broke, and if you'd wave your bridle at him, he'd come at you with his mouth wide open and slide right up to you. All you had to do was hold that bit out and he'd grab it in his mouth himself.

Well, Dad walked into the corral and the stud trotted around. Dad threw his hand up in the air to stop him and that stud run at him with his mouth wide open. I'm telling you, I didn't think Dad could get his fat belly between the rails on that corral, but he yelled, "What the thunder!" and slid out of that corral like a greased weasel.

First money at Lincoln.

Was he mad! I took his bridle and stepped into the corral, held the bit out in front of me and hollered at the horse. He ran up and grabbed the bit and I handed the Old Man the reins. He rode that stud from then on and was mad when the owner came to get him.

Another time a guy brought up five head to finish off. He said, "These horses won't need much riding because they are all gentle and no one else has fooled with them." They were gentle enough and halter broke. They were all tall, leggy and weighed 1,200 pounds or better, and I would say they were a Standard Bred cross, really nice saddle stock but they had age on them. The youngest showed five years and the oldest at least seven.

One was a mare, the oldest. When I put my hackamore on her, she just stood there. Next came my saddle and she didn't even move when I cinched it up. I turned her around and Gene says, "You'd better get a good seat in that saddle when you get on." When I put the reins around her neck and reached for my stirrup, all the muscles in her neck and body just tightened up. I hit that saddle and we were airborne. It wasn't long before I was stacked out on the ground and this old girl was still at it. Gene picked up the reins and took a seat. He had the same luck as I. We'd take turns on that Old Heifer. She was so strong and fast she'd buck so long she'd just plain poop us out.

Finally, one day Gene was up there doing a fine job when the rigging on his saddle broke. He turned over in the air with that saddle still between his knees and lit on his back. Gene jumped up, got another saddle on her and I'll bet she remembered that ride to her dying day. We kept after her like this and finally she allowed us to ride her and you were sure mounted whether it was a steep mountain or working stock. She was there with plenty of fire.

Well, we decided we'd work the other four out under a pack saddle during hunting season. This usually takes some of the salt out of them and

Me and an Arabian stud.

helps give them an understanding of bit. One day we were headed for the hills. I had 200 pounds of oats packed on each one of them and was riding this mare. We called her Buttons. When we unloaded at camp we held them in the corral all night and right after daylight I was headed back to the ranch, twenty-eight miles away. We'd loaded those four with over 200 pounds of bull elk quarters we had to get to the freezer.

As I said before, they were rank and long legged and could sure travel. I was on Old Buttons and she needed the work. I pulled into the ranch about 1:30, loaded them with 200 pounds of oats and headed back for camp again. We made it to camp after dark as I was needed there the next day to guide a hunter. Gene says, "Think it would hurt Old Buttons if I rode her to Basin tomorrow?" I said, "You can't hurt that mare. Might do her good as she still had plenty of steam when I got here tonight."

Well, next morning Gene saddles up for a trip to pack out a bull elk down in the Basin country. Now, Old Buttons, after two hard days and a half a night, stacked Gene out right in front of the cook tent. When she was twenty-one years old, you'd better talk to that old girl in the morning or she'd sure hand you a ride. Without a doubt, she was the best saddle mare I ever rode, if you could weather that first storm.

When you're riding out broncs or breaking saddle horses you never know what to expect. They're all different and different things work on one horse and won't on the next. Some are sulky and balk, just freeze up and you can't get them to move, while others move too fast and you can't stop them.

One time I was breaking a stocky, heavy-bodied bay for a neighbor and decided to ride him to town, seventeen miles away. Everything went well until I was headed home and trotting him up the old county road, when, Bang!, he stops, spreads his legs and froze up. I tried everything I knew to get him to move. No deal. He'd gone as far as he was going.

Sometimes you just sit quiet on them and wait them out and they'll get their mind off their troubles. Mebby a gopher or a bird flying by will change their mind, and away they'll go just like nothing had happened.

There was no changing Shorty's mind so I was just sitting on him waiting. I heard a car coming down the road and when it got to me, it was a neighbor with lots of years behind him and he said, "Having trouble?" I said, "I'm just waiting for this jackass to change his mind. He's balked and I can't get him to move."

This old boy got out of the Ford and started digging under the front seat. He came up with a harness ring about one and a half inches in diameter, walked over and grabbed the nag by the ear. He said, "Get set." I took a deep seat and gathered up the slack in my reins. He slipped that ring over that horse's ear and gave it a hard shove down to his head, popping the ring over the cartilage next to the horse's head. That old pony sort of twisted his head sideways, shook it a couple of times, and we left, headed for home. Up to just a few years ago, if you saw my saddle, there was always a ring tied in a saddle string where I could get it easy. I don't know how many times this has saved me a long walk home.

Age and experience is sure a good teacher.

Another time I was starting a big hammer-headed colt in the corral

Duke, a real draw.

when a car drove up and out stepped these two old boys from Deer Lodge. One of them said, "I'll bet you four bits you can't ride him clean." By clean he meant no horn pulling and spur as you did at rodeos. I said, "Put your money on that corral post," and stepped on. Now this pony was big, rank and wild. I'll tell you, if anyone ever earned a four bit piece, I sure did that time. That horse sure was a handful.

Now the other day a guy gave me this poem defining what a cowboy is. If I'd have seen it years ago, it sure would have saved me lots of aches and pains as well as hide. Here it is. Read it for yourself:

WHAT IS A COWBOY??
Author Unknown

Between the security of childhood and the insecurity of second childhood, we find the fascinating group of humanity called "Cowboys."

They come in assorted hat sizes, shapes, weights and stages of sobriety. They can be found anywhere....cities, towns, the wilderness, in bars, in jails, on the road and always in debt!

The hard way.

He is laziness with a deck of cards, bravery with a pair of spurs, energy on the dance floor, a legend of the Old West with a copy of Playboy and seldom without a case of beer.

He has the energy of a turtle, the slyness of a fox, the stories of a sea captain, the sincerity of a liar, the aspirations of a Casanova and when he wants something, it is usually connected with girls or horses!!! Some of his likes are: women, beer, girls, alcohol, females, booze, dames, firewater, the opposite sex, rodeo, dances and the smell of horse manure. His dislikes are: answering letters, his boss, officers, gettin' up on time and being told to take his hat off.

No one else can cram into a pocket...a little black book, a photo of his best girl, a pack of crushed cigarettes, a hoof pick, a book of matches, a can of snuff, a comb, a beer opener, and what's left of last week's paycheck. He likes to spend some of his money on girls, some on poker, some on beer, some on shooting pool and the rest for foolishness.

A cowboy is a majestic creature! You can lock him out of your house, but not out of your heart. You can scratch him out of your little black book, but not out of your mind. You may feel like giving up on the leery-eyed, good-for-nothing, long-away-from-home lover boy, but all your shattered dreams become insignificant when your Cowboy knocks on your door, looks at you with those blood-shot eyes and says, "Hi Honey!"

FANNY SPERRY STEELE & TRIXIE

Fanny Sperry Steele was born Fanny Sperry back in the 1890's, somewhere around the Gates of the Mountains. She learned to ride before she could walk, as the story goes. Like most ranch kids she was taught to ride a horse bareback, without a saddle, and she developed a sense of balance that almost amounted to having glue on the seat of your pants. Fanny was one whose sense of balance outdid the glue by far.

She loved horses and loved to ride—had a way with animals that few people ever gain. She rode all the country from Wolf Creek, Helena and the Gates of the Mountains working cattle and horses from the time she was a tiny girl.

Finally she started breaking horses to ride at the home ranch and for neighbors and surrounding ranchers. At a very tender age she became an excellent bronc rider and rode a few local rodeos where she became noticed by circuit riders and producers.

As I remember her telling me, Bill Steele, a rodeo clown, was the person who talked her into going up to Calgary and entering the ladies bronc riding contest. This, I believe, was in 1914.

Now she had to ride against all the lady riders of the time.

The ladies' bronc riding contest was run under different rules than the men's. Ladies would hobble their stirrups, tying them together with a rope under the horse's belly or to the cinch. This would hold the stirrups solid and not allow them to swing as the bronc bucked. Much easier to ride a horse this way as you could hold your stirrups on your feet better. No deal! Fanny would not ride this way. She rode them slick just like a man.

To contest you came out of the chute with your spurs in the horse's shoulders and spurred both forward and back as the horse bucked. The ladies did not spur their horses.

Well, Fanny came out with one hand in the air and her spurs flashing from the shoulders to the back of that saddle and won the World

The Lady Fanny on Midnight, 1915.

Championship Ladies Bronc Riding honors.

She also told me of riding Midnight, the top men's saddle bronc of the time. Only one or two men ever rode him in his long life.

In her words, "He was one of the roughest broncs I was ever on and I would not have ridden him if I had not D-ringed him."

Now D-ringing is when a horse is about to throw you, you'd grab your spurs into the cinch, giving you a solid hold with your feet and legs. You also would grab the horn (pulling leather) because, with your spurs hooked in the cinch solid a horse would beat you half to death if you couldn't hold your body solid, not allowing it to whip back and forth as he bucked and turned.

She always claimed the roughest bronc she ever rode was Old Steamboat, a big bay horse from Cheyenne, Wyoming. Her words were, "He took the bronc riding out of me."

Fanny and Bill got together a rough string and tried rodeo producing for a while, but as she told me there was no money in it and they had to trail their stock too far, so they gave it up.

This is when they came to Arrastra Creek on the west side of the divide and bought a little ranch. They raised a few cows and Pinto horses and started an outfitting business. They packed hunters and fishermen into the Lincoln back country and sometimes the South Fork of the Flathead country, now the Scapegoat Wilderness area and the Bob Marshall Wilderness area. Fanny did most of the packing as by this time, Bill was

Fannie Speety Steele on Brahma Steer. Bozman

She liked cows, too.

having health problems.

I don't believe she ever guided these hunters. She furnished the camp and packed them in and their game out, sometimes cooked for them. She did a good job and they all loved her. I never heard a soul ever say a bad word about Fanny.

She was a wonderful cook. If you happened to stop by her place and the kitchen door was open, you could smell fresh bread baking. She could bake the best homemade bread I ever ate.

I remember one time when Gene and I were hunting mountain lion and ended up at her place late one night in the middle of winter. We were a long way from home and on snowshoes. Us and our hounds were completely pooped.

Gene knocked on the door and when Fanny opened it, the aroma of fresh bread hit us in the face and almost knocked us down. We were starved.

She invited us in and set a cup of coffee out for us and said, "Could you eat some fresh bread?" Could we eat some fresh bread! I guess we did. I'm sure she had to bake again the next day.

To me she was always "The Little Lady with the Silver Spurs"—a very refined, small lady that stood ten feet tall.

We used to put on a rodeo at the ranch in the summer and I saw her ride exhibition at the age of sixty-five for $15.00. She also rode exhibition at big shows at this time for $25.00 and you should have heard

Fanny Sperry Steele—World Champion.

the cheers from the grandstands.

Finally, Father Time caught up to her and she had to move to Helena where she passed away, but not before she was nominated and accepted into the "Cowboy Hall of Fame" in Oklahoma City, which was a great honor to her and her family and friends.

It is too bad it happened so late in her life that she had no time to enjoy or see her place of honor in the museum.

There was another lady of rodeo that graced our community over the last years. She was Trixie McCormick of Ovando and parts unknown.

She was born in Stevensville, Montana, as Trixie Stokes. Her father was sheriff of the county, as I remember.

Trixie and her brother, Leo, were a rodeo team. Trixie was a trick rider and roper and Leo was a Roman Racer, riding two horses running at the same time. Sometimes he had three horses and stood up on them while they ran the race tracks.

Trixie and her horse, "Silver Dollar," won worldwide fame as a team, both in trick riding and fancy roping.

She would do all of the rope spinning tricks in the book. I saw her when she was near sixty years old standing on a table while spinning a sixty-foot loop around her and the table, then jump off the table and keep the loop spinning around her.

I knew her and Leo very well for I rode the rodeos with them.

Back in the 1930's the Calgary Stampede up in Canada was having a hard time surviving those Depression years and was about to fold up. A guy by the name of Guy Wiedick was the head producer of this big show

Her calling card.

and it was he who had hired Trixie to perform at all the shows.

While talking one day he said he was going broke. Trixie said, "Guy, if you'll pay my expenses and buy me the clothes I need, I'll put this show on the map again. You always put on a show for advertisement in Chicago and New York each winter. You book me and "Silver Dollar" at some theaters and I'll give you $5.00 for every $1.00 you spend advertising.

Guy says, "It's a deal."

Trixie was well put together at that time and she had fancy skin-tight pants and shirts made of silk with lots of shiny sequins sewn in the right places. Also in some of her rope tricks she wore skin-tight tights and very revealing blouses by standards of those times. She filled her clothes well.

I can remember the pictures in the papers and the radio commentators comments about this gal performing in such places as the "Madison Square Garden" in half nudity, but it sure put the "Calgary Stampede" on the map. In press releases advertising the stampede, Trixie was shown and Guy called her the cowgirl that brought sex to rodeo.

If you're ever by Ovando, you'll find Trixie's Bar just off the highway with many pictures of her in her heyday.

She always wanted to make a trip into the mountains with me and Steve, my son, when we were setting up hunting camp. Well, one year she went with us. One day I was taking a ride over some country to spot

Putting Calgary on the map.

game, etc., and Trixie and my wife, Marg, wanted to go along. I told them it was too rough a trip for them as I was not following any trails and part of the time we'd have to walk and lead our horses over steep, rough mountains. I'd guess about twenty miles would be covered. Trixie says, "I've known you a long time and I never saw the day you could outride me."

Well, away we went and covered some mighty steep country. Nobody bitched or bellyached a bit 'til we were walking down to the cook tent from the corrals. These two gals were kind of gimping along and I says, "You gals walk like you're stove up pretty bad."

Trixie says, "We're all right, but you never told us we'd have to ride with a horse's tail hanging over our eyes so long. That's steep country."

Next day we packed up and headed for home. On the way down the trail we met another outfitter packing hay into his hunting camp. We pulled off the trail to let him by and the horse Trixie was riding was in a big hurry to get home. He turned in to the moving string of mules. Trixie's foot hooked on a bale of hay and twisted it. I asked her if she was all right. She said it hurt but she was O.K. When we got to the corrals she limped a bit but I never thought much about it. She seemed all right when we dropped her off at home.

I saw her a couple of days later and she'd been to Missoula to see a doctor. She'd broken her ankle in that wreck and never griped a bit. I guess that's the kind of guts it took to make her a world champion trick rider in the years before.

Trixie and Silver Dollar.

Old Buttons and Dad.

COWBOY

Somewhere in the stories before this, I have mentioned my interest in being a cowboy. Well, it finally came to life along in the 30's. I was breaking horses for people to ride and found out I could do a fair job on a bucking horse. I decided I should try my luck as a bronc rider at the local rodeos. I scrounged up the necessary equipment needed - spurs, boots, a big hat and the rolling walk of a cowboy. I hit the Helmville Rodeo and Lady Luck was in my pocket. From there on I really built to it, entering in both saddle and bareback broncs, did a little steer roping and had a big time. Even "picked up" part of the time.

When you pick up at a rodeo you are mounted on a saddle horse and your job is to help the rider dismount without injury, so you ride in close to the bucking horse, grab his lead rope and the rider can grab ahold of you and your saddle, swing over your horse's rump and dismount with your horse between him and the bucking horse, eliminating getting kicked or run over.

One day at a rodeo me and my pal were walking over to the chutes. I was going to make my draw for the finals. Back then you drew a horse and, if you made enough points to be one of the top three or four riders, you'd draw for the finals. It would be a contest between the three or four best riders of the day. As we walked along, Claude said to me, "You're not going to enter against those Turtle riders are you? I said, "I don't know. I'm just thinking." The Turtles was the first professional cowboy association formed back in the 30's and in later years reformed and called National Rodeo Cowboys Association.

A group of these boys had just come down from the Calgary Stampede in Canada on their way to Cheyenne, Wyoming, and stopped at Helmville to pick up a few dollars as they went through. There was Turk Greenough, Bill Linderman, a guy named Roberts, and then there was also Bill Russell, a tough rider to beat.

I was telling Claude that I didn't know if I should ride against such professionals or not. I hardly got the words out of my mouth when someone slapped me on the back. I turned around and there stood Old Turk Greenough. He said, "Kid, I've won as much in this riding business as any man alive, and I never had to ride another rider yet."

That clinched it. I'd ride.

I drew and came up with a horse called "Gold Dust." She was a sunfishing spinner and could sure give you a ride. I'd drawn her before and she was my kind of horse. I had been the first man to ride her so I felt good. She came out of that chute bawling and sunfishing like it was her last chance at freedom. My timing was right and I lucked out with first money.

I've always had a big spot in my heart for Old Turk Greenough and Bill Linderman. They were not only great bronc riders, but guys that would help you and stick by you when you needed someone.

Some rodeos would put on what they called a "Mad Scramble." Everyone who entered in the show drew a ticket. This ticket was numbered and you were supposed to ride a saddle bronc, bareback horse or a steer in the mad scramble. The animals were numbered and you had to take the animal that matched your number. No choice. Usually, there'd be four saddle broncs in the bucking chutes, five or six barebacks in a long cow chute and some steers in another. You rode with your heart in the seat of your pants, I'll tell you. They'd turn everything out at once, steers, broncs and barebacks. You either rode or got run over. I always figured, if I got throwed I'd be a one-armed cowboy or I'd have a muley saddle, no horn left.

I knew a couple of these old boys who really loved this life along with Old John Barleycorn. Well, they were at a show in Augusta, Montana, one time. They had partied along the way coming so were late getting to town; also feeling no pain, and in a playful mood, we'll say. There was only one hotel in this fair city and all rooms were taken. Well, they went upstairs looking for some friend to hole up with when they came upon this room with one drunk in it. He was passed out cold. They shook him and couldn't rouse him, so they picked him up and carried him out the back way and laid him in the alley. Then they called the undertaker and told him to pick up this dead guy behind the hotel, claiming they were the sheriff of Cascade County. Well, he sent his hack and they loaded the guy in it and bid him goodbye. They both told me they never seen the drunk again, but the undertaker said the guy was sure enough mad and looking for them and some scalps when he came to.

One of these boys won the world champ bronc ride in Madison Square Garden a year or two after this and the other went down in the Cowboy Hall of Fame in Oklahoma City.

Back then they had a concoction they called "Hokey Pokey." You'd mix up some of this and that in a bottle, shake it well and put a few drops on the rump of a cow or horse that hung up in the chute, and he'd sure leave that spot in a hurry, bucking and kicking like he'd gone mad. It really didn't hurt, it just burned like a thousand hot needles for just a minute or two. I'll tell you how I know this.

At Helmville, Old Tom Geary always ran the steer chutes and he always had a bottle of Hokey Pokey in his pocket. He loved to catch a cowboy sitting on his saddle horse talking to someone. Then Tom would slip up and shake a few drops on that old horse's hind end. Now this unsuspecting lad would find himself making a bronc ride or flat on the ground with everybody laughing at him.

You sure had to watch when you got on your steer for your ride. They didn't have Brahmas then. We used three- and four-year-old range steers, big and they could sure hang and rattle. As I said, you'd better watch for Old Tom cause he'd hit the steer with Hokey Pokey and give you a shot too. Now, what the steer started to do to you, the Hokey Pokey would finish and you'd be on the ground doing a war dance. I know, because I've done that war dance. It sure increased the entertainment of the day but ruined your chance at the money.

Along about this time there were two clowns working the rodeo circuit who were always into some sort of shenanigans. What one didn't think of, the other did. They became two of the early-day bull fighters, as they were just starting to use Brahma bulls in the shows. Their names were Homer and Pinky, and they really became big names in the rodeo business.

Well, the story goes, they were on their way to Oklahoma City to a big show. As they drove along this road, a bobcat ran across the road and up a tree. One of them roped this cat and they dumped all the clothes out of a suitcase and put the bobcat in it. When they got down the road where the traffic was heavier, they stopped and laid the suitcase in the road, then hid and watched.

Along came a car with a bunch of young guys in it. They drove by the suitcase, stopped and backed up. Then an arm slid out the back door and grabbed the suitcase. Well now, that car hadn't gone far when it went crazy on that old dirt road, ending up tangled in a barbed wire fence. The doors flew open and out flew four guys end over end, then out came the bobcat and headed for parts unknown. I've heard this story told by a dozen different cowboys who swore it to be a fact. Knowing them, I, for one, can just see them laughing as they sacked that cat.

Another time I was riding at a rodeo in Lincoln, Montana. The show was put on by a guy who was a trick roper as well as a rodeo producer. His wife was a Roman rider. He had rented all the stock from local ranchers. Joe Hooper had some Arabian cross colts, three- and four-

Go West young girl and get a horse.

year-olds running up in the hills with this Pinto stud, which was half Arab. They were all small horses, wild as elk, but sure could buck, and were faster than greased lightning. It was a two-day show and this stud had thrown his rider each day. As the show was closing the announcer offered to pass the hat for anyone who'd take a setting on this pony. There was a big crowd and, as I watched people dropping money in the hat, I figured I was just the guy for this job. Going up to the chutes, I claimed a seat on this nag. While the chute boys were saddling him, I was getting ready. I had a sip or two of that encouragement medicine one of the boys had. Mebby one sip too many.

Anyway, out of that chute we came. I'm sitting up there doing fine and when the whistle blew I just stepped off that old pony easy like. When I hit the ground, I landed on a round rock. It rolled and so did I. I sure hit the ground hard, full length. I dislocated my hip, broke my left arm and lost a lot of skin. Gene and another guy pulled my leg, popping my hip back in place, and a doctor in the crowd set my arm and splinted it.

When I got back to pick up my money, there was sixty-seven cents in the hat. Some of the boys let me know that the producer had left early in the afternoon with all the gate money, so no pay for the riders, ranchers or the city of Lincoln, who had done all the work for him putting on the show. They said some of the riders thought he had headed for Salmon, Idaho, and were after him, but they were wrong. He didn't go that way.

Back then this was not an uncommon thing to happen at rodeos and horse races, too. Some sharp guy with lots of personality and a slick tongue would put on a show in some small town, hiring local men and women to do all the work, lease the stock from local ranchers, promise much to the city fathers and then when the show was about over, he'd take all the gate money and disappear, leaving contestants, workers and ranchers to hold an empty sack.

Riding in the high country.

REMOUNT - FAIRY BASIN

In 1937 the weather was so dry you couldn't dip a bucket of water out of a well. Hot and windy all over the Northwest. Idaho, Montana and Washington was burning up with forest fires.

We got a call from the Forest Service and they needed packstrings to fight fires. Gene was in the South Fork of the Flathead with one string. He had a surveying crew for the Forest Service so it was up to me to take the other string on the fires.

The Forest Service sent their trucks up after me and the packstring. When we arrived at the Nine Mile Remount and started to unload the stock, a crew of horseshoers started shoeing them. There must have been six shoers in the crew because as fast as we led the stock out of the truck, someone would lead them into the blacksmith shop and they had them shod so fast it was almost unbelievable. Two blacksmiths fit the shoes and five or six shoers nailed them on. Then all my stock was put in a pen by itself.

As I remember, there were twenty-seven private strings and ten government strings. Each string consisted of nine pack animals and a saddle horse. Each string was given a special pen on each side of an alleyway leading to the loading chutes. When a siren would sound, it meant there was a fire someplace and a string was loading. When the first string went out, your string was moved up until you were in the number one place and your name would come up on a board in the bunkhouse and at the loading chutes so you always knew who was to take the next fire call.

When that siren sounded, you'd grab your sleeping bag and duffel and run for the truck being loaded. I would say, at the most, you'd have five minutes from the time it sounded 'til the trucks were rolling out the gate. You never knew where you were headed until you got down the road and asked the driver. The trucks were called Gondolas and hauled ten head of horses and mules plus all your saddles and manti covers. It was sure a smooth run operation.

Major Kelly and Captain Evans were the bigshots, but the guy that really made it run smooth was Ed McKay who was in charge of men and livestock. He was, by far, the nicest and best manager I have ever worked for or with. I never remember seeing a load of stock loaded or unloaded that Old Ed was not sitting on top of the chute. No matter what time of the night your truck pulled up to those chutes Ed McKay turned on the loading lights. If you had a horse or mule with a gald or cinch sore, you had better have an explanation of how come. How he could remember all those horses and mules, I don't know.

There were around 375 head going in and out all the time. If a horse had a new spot or scale the size of a quarter, Ed knew it. You could just look at the man and you knew he commanded respect and he gave you the same at all times. If some hand didn't hold up his end at work, there were no words, he just wouldn't be at the table next meal.

We packed for fire crews in Montana, Idaho, Washington and northern Oregon that year. In Idaho at Avery on the St. Joe River, and the Mallard Creek fire, I spent almost a month from one fire to another. My truck driver's name was Jimmie Pierce, as crazy as any truck driver could be. He loved to go through a small town in the middle of the night, wide open and, when we hit the first buildings, he'd turn on the air horn and pull the siren wide open. I'll bet there wasn't a man, woman or child that didn't wake up. He'd say, "No sense in just us not getting any sleep."

Some of these roads were narrow, crooked and steep. The trucks were long wheelbase and on many a turn you'd have to back up and work that truck around them. Sometimes trees were rubbing both sides of the truck bed. I said, "Jim, I don't see how you get this rig up and down these roads." His answer was, "Just put her in the leastest and give her the mostest."

In Idaho, we had what they called dry lightning. You could have the awfulest electric storm with not a cloud in the sky. One night I had to camp up on Cider Mountain north of Avery at a lookout tower. Me and that lookout guy counted fifty lightning strikes that one night, and could count forty some fires burning all around us. If I remember, they claimed there were over a hundred fires that the snow put out that no man was ever to in northern Idaho and western Montana that summer.

Jimmie knew where all the public campgrounds were along the highway. When we were approaching one he would slow the truck down, and as he passed, he'd hit the air horn and siren. People would bail out of their tents and campers like a turpentined cat. He really loved it. This is why he drove trucks.

Now this St. Joe River is one of the most beautiful and spectacular streams I've ever seen in my life. It's rushing white water through high walled cuts, out into long deep pools of blue-green water, some of them so deep the water looks black, with white foam floating on top caused by the rapids between pools. The banks were lined with huge cedar and spruce trees. I've often wished I'd had a camera back then.

At Avery, Idaho, I was sent out to the Red Ives fire on the head of the Little Joe River. When I rode up to the fire camp, who's there but Old Scoop Skoval from the Flathead district and he's cargo man in charge of all packers and supplies. He said, "Throw your mantis over there and I'll give you a job where you don't have to manti your loads." Then he leads me around the supply tent and shows me all these wooden boxes. They were sixteen by eighteen inches and four feet long, all loaded with axes, pulaskies and shovels, each weighing over 150 pounds apiece. Me, I only weighed about 130 pounds at that time. You put two boxes to the mule and you had nine pack animals. Add it up. That's a lot of work. I'd stand those boxes on end, lean the bottom over against my belly, hook my belt buckle on the end of the box, then heave back, using my weight and throw the box up on the side of the mule, and throw my ropes on it and make my tie. Sometimes that critter would step over and I'd miss him. I'm telling you now, it sure strained your milk.

I didn't say anything and, after a few days, Scoop said, "I got a different job for you, kid. I'm going to give you the water haul." He told me to load those water cans. These were fifteen-gallon tin cans in a wood frame. They were light when empty and you hung one on each side of the pack animal. When I'd finished this, here he came with a funnel, a piece of garden hose about twenty feet long and a Ranch Romance magazine.

He said, "There's this little stream of water just a couple of miles this side of the fire camp. If you put this funnel in the hose, the other end in the tanks, and the funnel in the creek, the water will run right in those tanks and you'll never have to load them while they're full. Just lead up the next mule when the first one is full of water." "What's the magazine for?" I asked. "That's to read while the tanks fill up. Now something else. The first few trips, be late to camp 'cause those cooks are an ornery bunch, but if they don't have water the men fighting fire will raise hell with them 'cause dinner is late. After the first trip or two, you get there ten or twenty minutes early and you'll eat nothing but pie and cake." He sure was right.

Another time they called for help on the Tango fire in the Flathead and we sent two strings on that fire. Well, Wendell, my brother, took one string. Now, he was smaller than I and who should be the cargo man but Old Scoop. He aimed Wendell at those tool packs and Wendell must have told him where to go because I saw Scoop later that year and he said, "You know that brother of yours, Wendell, is a hell of a lot smarter than you."

Now, like all places that hired a lot of men from all over the country, the Forest Service Remount sure had its share of characters working there. I'll write of some of them right here.

There were these two blacksmiths that worked for the Remount part-time. Dave would build all the horse and mule shoes during the winter, then run the shoeing crew in the spring. Usually, after the roundup in the spring at the Fairy Basin Ranch, they would shoe everything before they shipped the strings out to outlying districts.

Dave was an artist with a hammer and a hot piece of iron. He made all his own tools, nippers, pullers and pritzels; anything he needed. Jeff was a top blacksmith and shoer, too. They were both short, heavyset men with arms like a horse's leg, really big, tough men. What a pair to draw to.

They were jealous of each other and real enemies. They'd work all day together and fight each other that night. When they'd come into Missoula after a shoeing job, they would head for Ralph Kilburn's Hawthorn Bar on West Front Street for a beer. One would take a stool at each end of the bar, not speaking a word to each other.

Now, as they drank a beer, they'd move down the bar a stool, have another drink and move down another stool. Pretty soon there'd be only one or two stools between them, and they would be feeling no pain. By this time, all the other customers had taken new seats, giving the two of them lots of room. One of them would look at the other and say something unregrettable, and the battle was on.

Nobody would try to stop them, and I never heard of one whipping the other. They'd beat the hell out of each other for a while, then stop and look at each other. The bartender would set up a drink for each of them. They'd get up on a stool and call for another beer, changing stools every drink 'til they reached the end of the bar to the stool they started out on. They'd finish off their beer, get up and go home. This happened regular about once a month. What a pair they were!

It rained hard all over the country and no fires, so they sent a bunch of us packers down to Fairy Basin Ranch to build a hayshed. There were eight or ten of us. Along with us was Frenchy, the cook.

Now Frenchy was a ornery little guy, kinda like a Pekinese Poodle, always looking for a fight and couldn't do much about it. Then there was this big guy, Ben, who was head of the CCC boys camp at the Remount. He was given the job of boss on this job. He was always ready to accommodate Frenchy and the night or two before he had worked Frenchy over pretty good at the Nine Mile House so Frenchy was still owly when he got up to cook our breakfast Sunday morning.

He glanced out the window of the cook shack just as a car drove up in front and saw big Ben driving it. Frenchy grabbed a big pan of eggs he had just beat up for scrambled eggs at breakfast, and stepped over behind the door. As the door opened and a big man came in Old Frenchy tipped that pan of eggs over his head and yelled, "I'll get even with you, you son of a _____." Now this guy knocked the pan off his head and there stood Ed McKay, the big boss, in his Sunday best suit and eggs running down all four sides. Old Ben was standing on the porch laughing his head off. Well, right there we lost our cook and Ben lost his bossing job for thinking it was funny.

Now, I've already mentioned Ben, so I must tell you about his hitch as a baseball umpire.

Ben was in charge of all the CCC boys at the Remount and they had a hardball team playing all surrounding local teams on Saturdays and Sundays. Ben was their coach.

He decided the packers should make up a team also. Sometimes between forest fires we'd sit for several days with nothing to do but just wait.

We formed a team and as pitcher we had a tall slim guy by the name of Makee who hated Ben with a passion—Ben being a guy with a big, loud mouth and not much gray matter upstairs.

Anyway, one Sunday we took on the CCC boys team in a game. We did not have an umpire so Ben volunteered his services.

We are beating the boys pretty bad when Ben called a strike on Makee and put him out, with undue loud-voiced abuse. Makee said nothing, just walked up to Ben with his bat in hand and hit him over the head.

Well, they packed poor Ben off to the doc in Missoula where he came to. Next day he showed up with a bandaged head resembling a Turkish Sheik, proclaiming what he'd do when Makee came back from the fire he'd been sent on. When Makee returned, no one could find Ben, but as soon as Makee was called out on another fire, Ben would show up looking for him.

I'm sure he's never found him to this day.

Riders in the back country.

THE SWEDES, DANCING JACK, AND JOE GOULASH

I must tell you about the "Terrible Swedes." They came into Ovando one day in the 1930's and rented an old house west of town. There was Carl, the old man, two sons, and a daughter in her early teens. I believe they came out of the logging camps of northern Minnesota or Wisconsin, I don't remember. Carl's wife had passed away a short time before.

Now, these boys really liked Old John Barleycorn and never seemed to get enough of it. If it was in a bottle, they figured it was meant to be drank. When the daughter got to be about sixteen or seventeen years old, she could stand it no longer and ran away from home, back to Minnesota.

These three men worked in the logging camps here for many years. The boys were heavy equipment operators and Carl was a jack of all trades. I have never seen a carpenter like him. Give him a saw, hammer and nails and a few boards and he could build anything, even when he was drunk.

One time we were building a big cook house and bunkhouse at a sawmill. Me and another guy were trying to fit the quarter round around the ceiling and couldn't get our corners to fit that had to be cut on a 45 degree angle. Old Carl walked into this big dining room and picked up a piece of quarter round material and said, "You guys stay up there and nail it in place." He'd look at the corner, lay the quarter round on his knee and saw it off, then hand it up to us. Every piece fit perfect. He never measured anything, just looked and cut. We did that whole building and I don't think he made over two or three mistakes.

Along with loving to get drunk, they loved to fight. If they couldn't find anyone else to fight with, they would fight each other. Now, this wasn't play. They were big, strong, tough and very well scienced.

Usually, there was a dance at the town hall every other Saturday night. Well, the Swedes would always be there, most of the time spent at the Bucket of Blood Saloon. There were fights every night. The people got tired of it and demanded the county sheriff to send a deputy over from Deer Lodge to keep things straight on the dance nights.

Well, the sheriff sent this big, dumb kid over the next dance. When he arrived, he walked into the Bucket of Blood where the Swedes were having a party. One of them looked up and said, "Look what we've got boys." They grabbed that poor deputy, handcuffed his hands behind him and stuck a bottle in his mouth and poured him full of whiskey, just like you'd drench a horse for colic. They pinned that silver star on the seat of his pants and brought him down to the dance hall, paraded him around amongst the dancers, then back to the bar. By this time the deputy was in the same shape as they were. It wasn't so hard to get him to have a drink with them now. Everybody left them alone as they were just having fun. No one was getting hurt. Some thoughtful person called the sheriff and when he got there, all four of them were sound asleep in a big pile in the corner of the bar. The sheriff and his new deputy loaded all four in the cars and took them to Deer Lodge jail to sleep it off. This didn't slow up the Swedes at all.

One winter when Carl was working for me and my brothers at our sawmill, there was a big party and dance going on at the hall. The Farm Ladies put on a big feed in the community kitchen. It was some kind of annual deal every winter. All the help from the mill took an old car we had and headed for town. I was helping play music for the dance that night and saw that our mill crew and the Swedes were feeling no pain by suppertime.

The next morning, shortly after daylight, one of the boys from the mill came driving up to my house and said Old Carl was dying, that I'd better get him to a doctor. I jumped into my car and picked up my brother as I passed his house and went to the mill. When we got there Old Carl was laying out on the porch heaving his head off and the snow all around was just big purple spots where he had vomited. We finally figured out what was wrong with him.

About that time in years, Phillip's 66 had come out with a new antifreeze made of alcohol and put a purple coloring in it. Alcohol boils at a low temperature in your radiator so you always carried a jug of it in the car. If you had to buck deep snow very far your car would heat up and boil some out, so you carried a spare jug in the car or trunk.

Well, on the way home Old Carl had decided he needed another drink. He could find no whiskey, but he found this jug of antifreeze. It looked good to him and he'd drank about a quart of it on the way home. It didn't kill him, but it sure laid him out for a few days. It almost put the big cure on him because he didn't get drunk for two weeks after that dance.

All of them have passed on now, but I'm sure telling you everyone knew they were here at that time. They were the best workers and really good at whatever they decided to do—even roughing up some poor bystander.

Then there was a guy we all called "Dancing Jack." He was a real dandy. He'd always show up at Helmville dances. I had a little dance band and furnished music for a lot of the surrounding dances, so I got to see it all.

When we had a dance at the Helmville Hall, Jack would spend the early hours at McCormick's Bar and down at Ed's Bar. Then around midnight you'd hear someone scream and in the front door of the hall would come Dancing Jack on a run. When he hit the dance floor, he'd do a couple of back flips, then go into a series of cartwheels, ending up in front of some poor unsuspecting girl on the sidelines.

He'd grab her and throw her around the floor 'til she was dizzy, then grab another and away he'd go. Dancers would clear the floor and let him have it. Now, many of these gals would hunt someplace to hide because he sure shook the curl out of their hair. All the time he was dancing, he'd go into these cartwheels and back flips and catch that gal before she could make it to a safe spot.

When he ran out of girls, he'd put on the greatest tap dancing you ever saw, then let a squall out of him and cartwheel out the door and you'd never see him again that night unless you went to the bar.

I've often wondered why he spent his time pitching hay to a cow because he could do anything on that dance floor that Fred Astaire thought of.

Old Jack is gone now, but there is many an old-timer that still tells tales about him. I'd have given and eye and tooth to have been able to dance half that good.

Then there was Old Joe Goulash who had a cabin and timber claim up in Deer Park. He was a nice old guy, had a Spanish American War pension and did nothing but trap bear in the spring and sell their pelts.

He'd walk every place he went, travel from one ranch to the other all summer and fall. When Old Joe showed up at a ranch, the first thing he did was to run the lady of the house out of the kitchen and he'd take over the cooking and dishes. What a cook this old boy was. He always had hot rolls, biscuits or bread. He claimed bread was no good after it cooled out.

Also, when he showed up he'd be carrying a long bamboo fish pole over one shoulder and a basketful of trout as a gift.

Now he might stay overnight or a week, you never knew. When he was ready to get to the next place, he'd put his hat on, pick up his fish pole and be gone—never say where, why or goodbye.

One day he walked into the ranch, peeled off his hat and coat and gave my Mom the bums rush out of the kitchen.

Mom said, "Don't you want me to put the fish on ice?"

Joe said, "No fish, Missus. Next time."

He acted kinda funny so Mom said, "What happened?"

Joe said, "I'm a come up from the river on a game trail to a little flat where the huckleberries are and there's a baby bear sits on she's butt right in my trail. I'm hit her with my fish pole and she's let out a beller. Then her mama she's come at me from behind. I'm climb a tree and she's a set down and eat all my fish. When she takes her baby and goes, I don't have time to catch some more."

One time Joe decided to visit Bert Mannix and Gus Hoephner ranches, so he spent a lot of time catching enough fish for both places. Said he had about forty-some trout. Now as he's walking down the county road, along comes the game warden. Old Harry Morgan stopped to give him a ride. As they are going along, Harry asked him where he was headed.

Joe said, "I'm taking some fish to my friends, Bert and Gus. Goin' to stay a few days."

Harry said, "How many you got?"

Joe said, "A few."

Harry took a look and when he saw all those forty-some fish, he arrested Old Joe because not only did Joe have too many fish, he didn't have a fishing license.

When they got to Helmville, they stopped at Mike McCormick's bar, and while Harry is talking to Mike, Joe tells a friend if he wanted some fish to help himself, but put some rocks in the pack.

Well, they left for Deer Lodge and when they got there, they stopped to eat at a cafe. Joe saw another friend and told him to help himself to the fish, but put some rocks in the pack. Everybody knew Old Joe. After they'd eaten their lunch, Harry took Joe up to the courthouse to the judge.

The judge said, "Where is the evidence?"

Joe said, "Right here, and dumped the rocks and two fish out of his packsack. Poor Old Harry lost his case and the judge made him buy Joe's supper before he drove him back to Helmville. Old Joe loved to tell about this free trip to Deer Lodge.

BIG GAME

People ask me what differences do you see in the wild game in this area since you were a kid. I'd like to expound on this question for a page or two.

First of all, it's not just game. It's people and environmental changes that have affected all game animals.

Back in the 1880's, the settlers of this area found lots of elk, deer, mountain sheep and mountain goat through this whole mountainous area.

Some old-timers claimed to have seen over 1,000 elk feeding on Kleinschmidt Flat at one time. I've seen several hundred, but not that many. I have to believe them because of lush summer range and, at that time, an abundance of winter range to the west and south. They also told me of mountain sheep on Ovando Mountain and the Cooper Lake Range. I never saw them. Mountain goat, yes, but not sheep this far west of the Continental Divide.

When we first moved to the Tait Place on the North Fork, there were very few whitetail deer in the area. Along the river on Matt and Antone Jacobsen's, the Tait Place and up and down the river bottom there were a few whitetail, also the little fantail deer, a dwarf whitetail. Up on Ovando Mountain and Cooper Lake Range, there were quite a few muleys. They used to winter along Dry Gulch and the open hills down the Blackfoot River.

When it came to elk, they were few and far between. Most people hunting elk would go into the Danaher or down the South Fork of the Flathead. There had been big forest fires all through this area a few years before and, as I see it, that was the low ebb in the elk because they started to show up real fast in the next few years. Ovando Mountain, Monture and the Cooper Lake Range really came back to good elk and deer feed. Spring Creek under Ovando Mountain had a big natural salt lick and so did McDermott Creek above Coopers Lake.

Right about this time Joe Murphy was having a hard time finding elk at White River on Murphy's Flat. I remember him telling of having to move camp up White River to Brushy Park to find any elk for his hunters. Now, this guy knew how to hunt elk and had been hunting the country since 1909. If there was elk there, he'd have found them.

Along about 1926 or 1927 we started to notice a big increase in elk and mule deer both. From that time on they just seemed to explode in numbers. Then came World War II with not many hunters hunting and this gave them the push that spread elk everywhere.

In the late 1940's and 1950's most ranchers were having elk problems in the wintertime. A bunch of elk can sure raise Cain with the haystacks. It got to the point where everyone built elk-tight hay corrals or haysheds sided up or the elk ate the hay. It was during this time that we would fence all our haystacks but two and let the elk have them. If you didn't, you were always fixing fence. Joe Murphy did the same where he was feeding 200 head or better. We only had ninety head.

About this time the Jacobsens were really having trouble with the whitetail deer. They had feed troughs to feed grain to their registered cattle and the deer would hop up in the feeders and eat the grain and chase the calves and bulls away. Finally, the State Game Department trapped a lot of whitetail deer and transplanted them all over the state, relieving some of the pressure from the deer problem.

Hello, my friend.

Boy, was there a bunch of mad people when the "Fish and Game" started trapping those deer. "All they're going to do is transplant our deer for someone else and kill them doing it." These were the words on many a sportsman's lips at that time.

Well, whitetail deer are like weeds when they get started. Today you can still hear the cry, "Got to do something about these damn deer." We have multiple deer tags and five weeks of rifle season plus the archery season. Looks all right to me.

Elk used to be different. They'd winter out here in the ranch country and as the snow receded, they would head back into the Scapegoat country, also up Monture Creek and back into the Bob Marshall Wilderness area.

Back then 99 percent of the meadowland was wild grass or timothy and clover mix that you would class as wild grass hay. Now we have lots of alfalfa, orchard grass, and alsike clover, most all irrigated. It comes up lush and green after haying. Also there are a lot of grain crops that make plumb good elk food. Especially oats, they really like a diet of this.

Then there are a lot of large ranchers, smaller ones, too, who do not allow any hunting along with the Clearwater Game Range. All of these areas provide a sanctuary for elk. Plenty of food and no one bothering them. Why should they go back and climb steep mountains and paw deep snow. If you put all of this in the right perspective, you'll see why the back country is a little short on elk.

When it comes to mule deer, I think they are a little different because we used to have so many of them from the tops of mountains to the floor of the valleys. I've driven past Markham Mountain in a team and sleigh and counted over 600 muleys wintering on the bare-faced sidehills. I know from what I've seen that whitetail deer will drive them out of certain areas.

In 1949 we had a terrible winter and lost a lot of elk due to winterkill in the back country. Mebby it's just taking them a long time to build up again. Also, mebby the fires of '88 will rejuvenate their range and make a difference. We hope so.

There is another line of thought. As everyone knows, it's the old cows that lead the migration. For years the cows were 100 percent protected in the back country, but in all the outlying areas they were not. Now, my thought is that when these old lead cows showed up out here on Monture, Ovando Mountain or Markham Mountain, did they get killed by hunters, leaving not enough old cows to keep the young elk migrating back and forth? Don't laugh. Just think about it. At least, to my limited experience of late, I believe I can see more migration starting in the last three years. I hope I'm right. Nature sure has a way of taking care of her own.

Spike camp on Dry Fork.

With the protection we are now getting on the bulls through the brow-tined law forced by the sportsmen of Montana, I, personally have great hopes for the future of the elk in this area. I don't believe you can have big bulls if you don't have young ones.

There is one herd of elk in the state of Montana that really astounds me. That herd is the Sun River herd. It has gone through all the ups and downs of weather, hunting pressures and persecution any herd could possibly get and yet it has expanded and never had to be restocked. The offspring of this herd has helped bolster the Scapegoat Wilderness area and the Bob Marshall Wilderness area and all places in between, while also supplying ample hunting for many hunters.

The Sun River Game Ranches have contributed so much more than the average sportsman realizes and this was dreamed of by one man and his ability to convince a small few others to get the job at hand done. Robert F. Cooney of Helena has written a tribute to this man that he has given me permission to insert here.

BRUCE NEAL: A Man and an Elk Herd
The Long Search for Winter Range in the Sun River Country
By Bob Cooney

It was sparkling cold that winter day in 1949. We had snowshoed quietly through pine covered foothills. Behind us rose the great escarpment of Sawtooth Mountain.

From a ridgetop where we rested we caught a glimpse of rolling grasslands that stretched beyond us to the east. Out there were well over a thousand elk. The majority were cows and calves with a sprinkling of spikes. Around the fringe of this big band we could make out small groups of mature bulls. Many were feeding, others were already bedded down.

It was a thrilling sight.

We were watching a part of the nationally famous Sun River elk herd. They were peacefully grazing on the 20,000 acre winter range northwest of Augusta, in Lewis and Clark County. This land had been purchased for them by the Montana Fish and Game Commission.

I was trying to visualize the thoughts that were going through the mind of my companion.

A well-worn Scotch cap was pulled down over his ears. A small black scarf was knotted about his neck. Gray-blue eyes were shaded by heavy brows. His rugged but kindly face was tanned and deeply lined by years of wind and rain and snow. His breathing caused frozen vapor to drift up into the cold air to form frost on the edge of his cap.

Resting there on his snowshoes, he presented the rare picture of a man perfectly at home with the rugged environment in which he had spent his life.

This was Bruce Neal, forty-three years ago.

I was sure that what we were watching must have been a thrill for him. Years of struggle to maintain this herd, against tremendous odds, had been at last climaxed by the purchase of the game range.

I had known Bruce for many years. Because of this, I felt I could guess something of his thoughts.

As a young man he had worked his way up along the Missouri Breaks and into the Augusta area. He had trapped wolves. Later he took up a homestead in the Upper Sun River Canyon, an area now covered by Gibson Lake. With a friend, Ralph Allan, they had operated a hunting camp. It was one of the first in that part of the Rockies. They guided hunters into remote areas of the Upper Sun River mountains, now the Bob Marshall Wilderness. They also packed across the Continental Divide into the Flathead country, often following vague game trails.

With the completion of Gibson Dam they were flooded out. Ralph Allan and his wife developed the K-L Dude Ranch at the head of the lake, now Klicks. Bruce joined the Montana Fish and Game Department as one of the early wardens. His life became even more closely involved with the elk herd.

He knew that in the distant past elk and buffalo had been plentiful in these foothills and even down along the Sun River Valley. Elk wintered in those long ago days out on the prairie edge where we saw them that morning. But they had been gone from there for years; held back in the

Bruce ready for work. (Photo courtesy Carrie Reissing)

snows of the high country by the activities of man.

About the time Bruce joined the Department, a change was taking place in the herd. From scattered numbers, they began increasing rapidly.

In 1926 elk again appeared in the foothills, but many changes had taken place. Ancestral winter range had for the most part become livestock pasture land and fenced hay meadows. There was no longer room for the elk.

During severe winters large bands began to migrate out onto private lands. Pasture use and fence damage resulted.

The first herding activities were pretty wild and disorganized. The winter they started, several bands had moved out from the foothills, nearly to Augusta. Riders on horseback were shooting into the air, dogs were barking and elk running pell-mell back toward the mountains. In their fright they no longer jumped the fences but ran through them. A good many were injured.

It was obvious that this was not a very good solution to the problem. The Fish and Game Department then gave Bruce Neal the responsibility of developing a more effective program of herding.

Bruce used to tell us that it wasn't very difficult to move elk in the direction they wanted to go. To push them back into the deep snow was something else.

He knew elk like a rancher knows his stock. In herding there were things to do and things not to do. Bruce used to say, "Boy, when there is a north storm on, leave them alone. If disturbed then they are likely to run right down out of the mountains. When the storm lets up you can start moving them back."

In the deep snow herders couldn't use saddle horses. A great deal of the work had to be done on snowshoes.

I helped Bruce on these winter drives many times, so saw firsthand how he did it.

Getting into the right position to push several hundred head of elk back up their migration trails was not easy. You had to watch the direction of the wind so as not to disturb them prematurely. Bruce's intimate knowledge of the trails and passes used by the elk meant a great deal to the success of a drive.

Noise, when necessary, was made in several ways. Bruce often carried a cowbell in his packsack. He jangled it when he felt it would help. A rifle was also an important tool in herding. Elk clear across a canyon could be started in the right direction by shooting into a big rock or cliff face on the side of the band opposite the direction you wanted them to go. They didn't seem to pay nearly as much attention to the sound of the rifle as they did to the crash of the bullet hitting the cliffs above them.

During this work Bruce was quite often aided by sportsmen and

Elk on the winter range Bruce Neal worked to get. (Photo courtesy Montana Department Fish, Wildlife & Parks)

local ranchers. Additional Department people were moved in when needed. His two older sons, Bob and Dan also helped. They were raised to know elk like most ranch kids know cattle and sheep.

This herding program went on for seventeen long winters. Bruce and his helpers put in countless snowshoe miles. It was a difficult and far from pleasant job. Elk were constantly being pushed back into deep and often severely crusted snow. The objective was to hold them a minimum of one night's migration distance back from the forest boundary. This meant at least six to twelve miles into the mountains. The grasses of the foothills and prairie edge were out of bounds for them.

Even with all this hard work, elk would sometimes break out and move on to private lands.

Most of the ranchers were patient and understanding. There was, however, one landholder in the Ford Creek area who was especially concerned. He would not allow herders to cross his land in their efforts to keep elk off. To make matters worse, he advertised in the Chicago Tribune for machine gunners to come out and help him protect his property from elk. Although none came, the problem quickly received national attention.

He tried unsuccessfully for a number of winters to kill elk on his land, out of season. At last, in 1941, two old bulls drifted down onto a pasture near his headquarters. He killed one of them. As he had hoped, the case came quickly to trial. The Montana Supreme Court handed down a verdict in his favor. As I recall, it did specify that a landholder should notify the Fish and Game Department of any such problem, giving them a reasonable opportunity to take care of it. It was, however, an important precedent and added to the seriousness of the Sun River elk winter range situation.

There were other critical problems developing. Elk being held back continuously on limited winter range in the forest were causing heavy use of available forage back there. Soil erosion was becoming evident in some places. In addition, elk were forced to concentrate on vital mountain sheep range in the upper Sun River Canyon. Being larger and more aggressive, the elk took much of the winter forage. The bighorns were declining in numbers. Their future was becoming uncertain.

By the mid 40's it looked as though the Sun River elk herd would have to be drastically reduced, perhaps cut in half.

This was the bleak picture one Friday morning in 1948 when the phone rang in the Helena Fish and Game office. I happened to be there with the director, Archie O'Claire. The call was from Bruce Neal in Augusta. He reported that two adjoining ranch holdings in the Sun River foothills had just come up for sale. This land was located at the end of several major elk migrating trails. It was some of the finest winter range the elk had been trying to reach for so many years.

We agreed heartily with Bruce that to purchase this land and dedicate it to the elk would go a long way in solving one of the most difficult game management problems in the west.

Then came the catch...

The owners were aware of the importance of this land to the department. They felt, however, they would be unable to hold up the sale for the long period necessary to complete a state acquisition. Bruce also told us there were out-of-state buyers ready, and that the owners would only hold for the state for a few days. This once-in-a-lifetime opportunity was definitely slipping away.

I can well recall the frustration we felt in trying to come up with a solution. Archie called Tom Messelt, a sportsman in Great Falls. Tom became as excited as we were. He had also long recognized the vital need for winter range in the foothills.

He said he would call us back. When the call came there was news that would change the course of events for the elk herd.

Tom had been in touch with Carl Malone, a rancher out of Choteau. Between them they had made the down payments for the land. They would hold it for the slower acquisition of the state. We quickly got back to Bruce. He was jubilant. He said, "You really get to know your friends when the chips are down."

Bruce Neal (left) receiving award in the late 1950s for his work on the Sun River elk herd from Bob Cooney of the Montana Department of Fish and Game.

For the elk herd it was as though the sun had broken out from heavy clouds.

The response of the herd even during those first winters was especially satisfying.

The foothill and mountain canyons no longer rang with the frightening sound of clanging cowbells and the crash of rifle bullets against nearby cliffs. The relentless push of the herders had ceased. After years of harassment, historic elk migration trails to the peace and quiet of the lowlands were open.

The game range was quickly made ready for the elk. Interior fences were removed. A jack fence with a "jumping rail" along the top was completed around the boundary. This type of fence, although stock proof, presented no barrier to elk entering the area. Several smaller acquisitions were completed. Nearly 4,000 acres of Bureau of Land Management lands were dedicated to elk use. Scattered tracts of State school lands were leased by the Fish and Game Commission. In all, a beautiful unit of timbered foothill and rolling prairie of some 20,000 acres was set aside for the elk. They lost little time in reaching it.

A wealth of native grasses held them there during the winter months. Pine and fir thickets in the foothills afforded shelter from storms and nearby cover. Only a minimum of careful herding was found necessary to drive more scattered bands back onto the range.

It soon became evident that elk were quickly moving through the critical mountain sheep ranges up the canyon. They no longer presented competition for forage up there and the bighorns increased dramatically.

As another plus, the ranch on Ford Creek where the rancher had killed the bull elk changed hands. The new owner has proven to be one of the finest cooperators along the foothills.

Soon after acquiring the game range, we were visiting the area with the late Dr. Olaus Murie, an internationally recognized wildlife authority. I will never forget him saying, "You fellows in Montana have here one of the very finest winter elk ranges on the continent."

Bruce Neal was a perfect choice as the first manager of the area. All of us knew the joy he must have felt in being able, at last, to welcome the elk onto the range after all those years of holding them back.

Those were surely some of the thoughts that were going through his mind that winter morning, as we watched the elk peacefully grazing on their own range.

Few men have been given a more rewarding answer to the dream of a lifetime.

Bruce passed away some time ago. He will not be forgotten. That lovely place up there along the outer edge of the Sun River Mountains, dedicated to an elk herd, will always be a reminder of this man.

Thank you, Bob, for writing this tribute. No one but you could have described Bruce so well. We were good friends, but I did not know his inner feelings so well.

Thanks to all of you.

Bruce Neal was the greatest. We were friends for many years. When he was State Game Warden in the South Fork country, he used to visit us at our hunting camps often.

World War II came along and I was gone in the Navy for four years. The first summer I was home after the war, I had a big group of people on a summer trip around the China Wall and down the South Fork fishing. Well, as I dropped into the Moose Creek basin up under the China Wall, I spotted a smoke at the little lake, and rode over to say hello as we rode by.

Who was it but Bob Cooney, his wife, and Fay Couey and his wife! I was riding a snaky colt and when I rode up and we were passing the time of day, I said, "Bob, how's Old Bruce doing? I haven't seen him since before the war."

Just like that, a guy stood up and let a yell out of him and threw his hat under my horse. Now, needless to say, that was all that old-bald faced colt needed. He let a bawl out of him and sucked his head down between his knees and went straight up at the sun, then down through the rocks and timber, bucking, doing everything in the book to dump me. I finally got him settled down and rode back up to the fire. There was Old Bruce with his floppy old brown hat and he said, "Still ridin' ain'tcha kid?" What a guy!

Another time I hadn't had a shave for a week and neither had I seen Bruce for several years. Now, as I passed his place, I stopped to say hello. Bruce's eyes were getting bad about that time. When I walked up to him, he squinted at me and said, "Peers to me you've aged a bit and I ain't. What's your name?" Can you beat that!

Right here I want to pay tribute to two other men who gave their life work to the sportsmen of Montana, Bob Cooney of elk management and James McLucas of trapping and transplanting of big game animals. Every sportsman in the state and those from over the world should take off

The head of Moose Creek where Howard ran into Bruce Neal. (Photo courtesy U.S. Department of Agriculture, Forest Service)

their hats to these two dedicated men.

Once at a get together of outfitters and game department men, we were having dinner after a meeting. In our talk it got around to Bob Cooney and he said, "The best big game management is none. Just manage the people." I'm sure he was right. Govern the hunting pressure and they will take care of themselves.

Jim was head of trapping and transplanting for the state. He started mountain goat herds where they were depleted and extended the range of elk and deer, promoting the great areas of game we have in the state today. My thanks to you, all three, for helping to give to me, my son and grandkids what we have today.

Let's talk grizzly talk for a bit. I lived in the time of sheep in the back country; from the Dry Fork of the North Fork of the Blackfoot River south to the Big Blackfoot River and Lincoln, Montana, from the Dry Fork east to prairie country on the east slope of the Rockies.

These sheep men were raising sheep to make money, not to feed bear. You really can't blame them. If you were doing the same, you'd have felt the same as they—a good bear is a dead one.

Some of them had a man hired to do nothing but cut pack trails and kill bear. These men carried a bottle of strychnine and when he found a dead sheep or deer, he would poison the meat, killing every bear that ate any of it, also the coyotes and wolves.

Outfitters did the same thing. I knew those who poisoned the entrails of every game animal they and their guides killed. I argued with them over it many a time—told them they were also poisoning themselves by killing the game that supported them. The outfitters finally saw the light and quit.

Then the Forest Service stopped leasing sheep range in the area and this stopped the stockmen's part in it.

Back in the early 30's, if you saw one or two grizzly tracks in a hunting season, you felt you'd had a great season. Hunting pressure had nothing to do with the depletion of bear during this time.

Now we have more bear, many more than is realized by most people, throughout the Bob Marshall and Scapegoat country, and also the surrounding areas, than we had in the last sixty-plus years.

It just goes to prove what Bob Cooney said of game management is still true. Game will take care of themselves if people are managed.

To me, the mountains would cease to draw me if there were no grizzly bear left, just hills.

Folks, Montana is still here, "High, Wide and Handsome." Her economy is low. It always has been. Much has changed since I was a small boy, but the big sky, beautiful prairies, snow-capped mountains, rivers and lakes, gold, silver, fish and game, timber and coal are still here. She still

Jim McLucas transplanting goats in the early days. (Photo courtesy Montana Department Fish, Wildlife & Parks)

has a wholesome environment, clean air, clean water, big sky and friendly, hospitable people. You can't change the mountains or stop the great rivers.

It's still here to bolster the economy. We just have to find a new way to do it. Look up to the mountains. From them get hope. They'll never let us down.

Come see us sometime and feel it for yourself.

SLEW FOOT

Over many years in the outfitting business I have become good friends with outfitters from British Columbia, the Northwest Territory, Alaska, Idaho, Wyoming, New Mexico, and even Africa. In every man's game country I find there lives an animal that becomes a legend in its own right. They all seem to be equipped with an oversupply of grey matter and luck. They develop instinctive survival tricks and learn to use them, making them almost impossible to get a shot at. They seem to know when, why and where in all circumstances.

One such grizzly ranged our Scapegoat country for many years. He now graces my living room with his size and beautiful, long, furred coat, a full silvertip with a bald face and long, white claws—a trophy for any hunter, young or old.

In 1947, along in October, my brothers and I pulled into our Danaher camp in the Bob Marshall Wilderness Area just before dark with a party of hunters. What a mess! It was the most disastrous looking camp I have ever seen! We had about two inches of snow and could read sign very good. Tracks showed an old sow grizzly and her cubs or yearlings had paid us a nice, long visit. The cook tent looked like your mother's clothesline on a windy day, just holes and strips of canvas waving in the breeze. Pots and pans, dishes, grocery supplies—not eaten—scattered all over the ground, all mixed up with dirt and bear manure. What a mess! It sure looked like a late supper to me. The bunk tents were not much better. Sleeping bags and gear were scattered all over. The sleeping bags were in good shape. The bears couldn't figure out these new-fangled zippers or mebby they'd have slept in them.

Inside the cook tent we had a six-hole cook stove. It was upside down, ashes scattered all over the place. When we got it back in place and some semblance of a kitchen set up, and a cook getting supper, someone says, "What's this?" Now, stuck in a bolt hole is a long tooth and part of the jawbone of a bear. He must have bit the stove, hung his canine tooth in the bolt hole, and then broke it and a piece of jawbone off when he tore his head loose from the stove. On closer inspection, the tracks showed one of the cubs had a slewed track. Every time he put his weight on his left hind leg, his foot would turn the heel out to the left and his toes completely to the right, leaving a slewed track that no one who saw it could ever miss.

It seemed that from that time on, when that bear would hit any camp or cabin he came upon he would leave his "sign." Now if no one was home, he would clean out everything edible. Always you would find a slewed footprint, his trademark, and all kettles, canned goods and buckets would have only three canine teeth marks in them. Thus he gained the name "Slew Foot."

This way of life must have really suited Old Slew Foot because he set himself up a regular route, just like the milkman in a big city. He'd hit Ed Geary's camp on Bar Creek, then our main camp, the Danaher Ranger Station, and then our camp up the Dry Fork. From there he'd cross the Danaher Divide and travel down to Cooney Creek Cabin and hunting camps along the North Fork down to North Fork Ranger Station. His next stop was Monture Ranger Station and then back to our Dry Fork camp, a circle of 100 to 120 miles. Always you'd find fruit cans with three holes in them and a slewed bear track. If no one was home he'd invite himself in and eat anything from horse feed to syrup and raw spuds. He did not like apricots. He'd bite into them and leave the cans full on the ground. A real gentleman, he always left a sign for you so you'd not blame any other bear, a trademark everyone knew.

I've seen him in the summer when I didn't have a gun and the season was closed. He'd not even bother to get in a hurry to get out of sight, but, come hunting season, all you'd get was a, "woof," a flash of a silvery ghost and tracks leaving fast. I'm sure he carried a calendar.

As the years rolled by he became bigger, smarter and bolder. It seemed he feared nothing or anyone.

In late October one year we were getting ready to take our hunters out to the ranch, twenty-eight miles away, when someone said "Old Slew Foot was here last night." We'd had a light snow and sure enough there were his tracks. He'd gone right past camp and headed up the valley. When we got on the trail, sure enough, there was Old Slew Foot's tracks headed up the trail. He did not go by his regular route, but stayed right on the trail. When he came to the ford on the Dry Fork, it was frozen over. He just padded right on across. When he got to the middle of the river the ice must have been a little thinner because he broke through, leaving the perfect print of a bear's body in the hole in the ice. You could see how he sprang out up on the solid ice, shook himself and headed right down the trail.

Wendell and Gene, my brothers, said he surely had something on his mind because he didn't waver off the trail in more than 18 miles. Well, when we reached the lower end of the canyon and headed for the ranch, Slew Foot was still on the main trail and making tracks straight for Monture Ranger Station.

Now many road hunters park their vehicles at Monture and hunt the outlying country at this time of year. Well, Slew Foot got into a pickup truck and a station wagon, and tore all the seats and upholstery out of them, plus ruining a paint job. He had no luck on the groceries, so down went the door of the ranger station and, after a good meal, back over the mountain to our camp on the Dry Fork. Nobody home. Nobody saw anything but tracks and tooth marks and a mess called camp.

How many tents he tore up for me I don't know. He never used the door even if we tied it open. He must have liked the sound of ripping canvas; he always tore all four corners and a hole in the roof.

One year our local ranger, Horace Godfrey, talked his wife into spending Labor Day weekend with him at North Fork cabin. This is a very nice place. The cabin is right on the bank of the river, a very spectacular spot, heavy fir and lodgepole timber, high red rock cliffs and blue-green water dashing down over red and white rocks. It is only a short three-hour ride from the trailhead, and in September, it is beautiful scenery all the way, enhanced by the fall colors and golden needles of the tamaracks (western larch).

Now this gal was a little skittish about these wilderness trips, but she went along anyway. The inside of the cabin has cupboards along one side, a cook range, windows on both walls, a table and bunk beds along the end and the north wall. She insisted Horace close the shutters on the south side and sleep under the north window to insure no bear trouble that night. Horace spread his cot and sleeping bag below the window and settled down for a rest. Laughingly, he told her that her fears were unbased.

Well, along about midnight there was a crash of glass all over Horace, and suddenly there was a bear standing with its front feet on his chest. He let out a holler and hit Mr. Bear in the face as Mr. Bear retreated out the window backwards. By this time, his wife is dressed. There was no way she'd wait for him to get the horses. She headed for home. He told me this himself. They walked out to the car that night and he returned the next day to get his horses. Old Slew Foot had won again!

Shortly after this, when we got to our halfway camp on Cabin Creek, we found it in shambles. Two fourteen by sixteen foot tents and a kitchen fly were torn into ribbons of canvas hanging over a ridge pole, groceries and dishes strewn all over the ground, and a bag of hotcake flour

Howard with cape of Slew Foot.

was scattered over everything with a nice Slew Foot track in the mess.

We were just finishing setting up sleeping quarters when in rode Al Mullenax, a packer for the Forest Service. With him were the new ranger and a string of mules. It was raining by this time, and they just sat on their horses and talked about the nice warm cabin they had down the creek with plenty of food and dry bedding. Little did he know that I had come by it and Old Slew Foot had been there, too. What a mess! I insisted they eat supper with us when the cook called, "Come and get it." But, no, they said they'd ride on to the cabin and enjoy a leisurely evening and supper.

The next summer as I was riding up the trail, who should I meet but Al and the Forest Service string. He pulled out in a little park so I could pass. As I went by Al said, "He who laughs last laughs loudest." Then he rode on down the trail with a smile on his face; one great guy.

We also packed in a lot of concentrated cake or pellets to feed our mules and horses. These are made of ground alfalfa hay and grain mixed with molasses; they are very sweet and palatable to animals, especially bear. They just love it—just like a bunch of kids in a candy store.

Well, Old Slew Foot got to raiding our grain tent at the barn. To get to the cake he'd walk along the front of the manger, past the hay, right in front of the horses in the barn. Usually just the smell of a bear sends them wild, but they got so used to him they wouldn't stop eating the hay in the manger. The horses paid him no more attention than a big dog.

We built a platform up in a tree and put the cake up there but he'd manage to tear it down. Finally, he moved into camp. The cook would step out of the tent to throw the dishwater and he'd be right there. When some unlucky hunter had to visit the outhouse at night, Old Slew Foot would run him back to the tent. It got so serious that Steve and I and Joe, our cook, decided we had to get rid of him before someone got hurt or killed.

We had a light snow one night so Joe and I took after him the next morning, one of us on either side of his tracks. Round and round we'd go in this dense thicket just above the corrals and saddle tent. We tried to keep him between us and at the same time see each other so we'd not get into a jam. Slew Foot would double back and circle us and give us the slip without showing himself, slicker than a peeled onion! We got only a couple of glimpses of him all afternoon. When we gave up to cook supper, he was still not 400 yards from camp. You talk about an animal being slick, smooth and smart, this old boy had it all. He was old, mean and cranky and developed into a minus to anyone near. He grew big, brazen, dangerous and beautiful

Now this old boy had Steve, Joe and me about whipped. Finally he made a big mistake and let Steve, my son, line that old .338 up on him. However, he did not go down without a fight. Eight or nine slugs he carried before he gave it up.

To me the hills have not been the same, and I'm sure this goes for Steve. It was like losing an old friend that would dirty-trick you every time he got a chance and you loved him for it.

Wendell and friend.

CLAYT JOHNSON

This all had to have happened back about 1950.

Wendell and I decided to look for cat (mountain lion) tracks down around Joe Murphy's place as he had about 100 head of elk feeding on his haystacks each night and quite a few deer.

In the daytime they'd all head up Warren Creek for Ovando Mountain and spend the day in the heavy timber below the mountain along both forks of Warren Creek. We figured there just had to be some lion where there was such a big concentration of game.

When we got down just below the Old Dry Gulch School, we saw a cat track cross the road. It looked like it had been made the night before. So we parked the old Model A alongside the road, put on our snowshoes, as the snow was at least three feet deep, and we and the hounds headed north toward Ovando Mountain and Warren Creek.

His track followed the east ridge of Warren Creek headed for Downey Lake. There was lots of deer and elk sign along the way and we expected him to make a kill at every draw, but he just kept travelling and showed no signs of hunting. Just before he came to Downey Lake, he swung west and hit the big elk trail leading from Murphy's haystacks to the head of Warren Creek.

When he stepped into that elk trail, we lost his track. The elk and deer had it padded down just like cement. Also, so many elk and deer had walked over his tracks that the dogs could not follow the scent.

It was getting late so we decided to head for Clayt Johnson's cabin up at Martin Park, and spend the night with Clayt.

Now Clayt was an old bachelor who bought a little piece of ground and built himself a home on the bank of Warren Creek. He trapped a little and worked for the Anaconda Copper Mining Company in the summertime as a smoke jumper, helping spot and fight any local fire on the surrounding area.

Clayt was a great storyteller and was the only man I ever knew who always shot his elk, deer or what-have-you right behind the left ear at at least 400 yards. How he always managed to be on the left side of that game every time he never explained. Also, how he made that old 300 Savage hold such accuracy at that range, I don't know. He claimed to be the best hound dog man and mountain lion hunter in the whole Southwest when he was younger. I've often doubted that, and some of his stories, but it was fun to visit with him and he did love to hunt.

It was dark as the inside of a cow when we got there. Clayt says, "What you guys doin' up here?" We told him we were hunting cats. He says, "You should be over in Lincoln Canyon. There aren't no cats in this country. If there was, I'd have had them hanging on the wall."

Well, we had a bite to eat and sat around talking. We asked him where the biggest concentration of deer was and he says, "Over along Dick Creek in that heavy fir and spruce timber."

Next morning he straps on his snowshoes and says, "Give me the Airedale's leash."

Well, now, he didn't know it but when you hit a fresh cat track, Old Cheese, the Airedale, would knock you down, jump all over you trying to get loose, and go after that cat. He'd just go wild and you really had to thump on him to keep him still long enough to take the collar off of him.

Well, we had just come to the edge of the timber about 200 yards from Clayt's house and we crossed three fresh lion tracks travelling together. They were red hot and Old Cheese made about three loops around Clayt's legs with that dog chain and headed after those cats.

Poor Old Clayt's down on his back, snowshoes in the air, and Old Cheese is towing him like a toboggan. I grabbed Old Cheese and Wendell untangled Clayt and we turned the hounds loose. Old Clayt laid there in the snow cussing the dog and smiled as we helped him up on his feet. "Ain't that sweet music, boys?"

Well, the cats split and so did the hounds. Now we've got three dogs going three different ways, each after a cat of his own. We really didn't plan it this way. Wendell said, "You go after Blackie and Clayt and I'll see what Skippy's got, then we can look for Old Cheese."

I hadn't gone far when I topped a little ridge above Dick Creek and there was Old Blackie setting at the base of this big fir with her head in the air moaning those long, tree bawls. I looked up that tree. From where I stood I could look straight out in front of me and in the top of that 200 foot tree sat this lion with the sun glistening on her shiny copper coat, just like a big lamp in a treetop.

Right then I remembered Wendell had my sixshooter in his packsack. I waited at the tree for a long time thinking they'd hear Blackie

A natural beauty.

and come to us, but no luck. I knew if I went back to Clayt's house I'd find a gun. But would Blackie hold the tree that long? She was a young hound at that time. Finally, I took a long rope and tied it around her neck and then tied it to a tree so she could move around under the lion, but not follow me.

When I got to the cabin I found a gun but no ammo so back to the tree I went. On the way I ran into Wendell and Clayt looking for me. They had Cheese and Skippy so I said, "Turn them loose and they'll go to Blackie." And so they did, right fast.

When we came in sight of the tree, that cat was higher up the tree. Clayt said, "I thought you said you'd tied Blackie to the tree. She's loose now." Sure enough, she'd chewed that rope in two and was trying to climb that tree.

Wendell and I sure gave Old Clayt a bad time about his saying there were no cats in his country, and also for being too old to lead an Airedale pup.

We got three mature cats that day and many more in the same area in years to come, but none were as much fun as when Old Clayt was with us.

Another time my brother, Gene, and I went after a cat over in Deer Park, south of the ranch. It was a deep snow year. The day before I had picked this old tom's track up on Iron Mountain and followed him to where he dropped into Bull Canyon after a bunch of mule deer.

Now going into Bull Canyon on snowshoes in deep snow is tough; it's steep and has too many thickets. When a cat went in there, we'd wait for him to come out and head for better country south toward Markham Mountain and Deer Park—more game for him and easier travelling. It would usually take them about five or six days to get out of Bull Canyon and over on Markham Mountain.

We got a snow of about six inches on top of the old snow and waited a day or two for it to settle more solid. When we thought the time was right, we headed out for Markham Mountain. We finally picked up his tracks, but they had the last snow in them so we knew we were two days behind him. We decided to take the main ridge of the mountain and, if by the time we reached the south end where the deer were yarded, we hadn't hit fresh sign, we'd go home.

When you reach the south end of Markham Mountain, it drops off steep into Quartz Gulch and is open, windswept ridges. This day the snow was crusted out there and glazed over by the wind. Before we got

A big tom.

completely out of the timber, the hounds started to bawl. They'd picked up fresh lion scent.

Now mountain lion have special scent trees where they mark their territories and every lion going through does the same thing. This old tom had left his, made a swing out on the bald hills, and headed back over the top for Arasta Creek. The hounds said it was fresh, but we couldn't tell due to the six inches of new top snow. It had been below freezing and the snow was dry, looked fresh, but no way of telling for sure.

Finally, we decided to turn them loose and trust those dogs' noses. They went down over the top and into the east side of the mountain. It was real heavy timber and it wasn't long before we lost sound of our hounds. Now the only thing we could do was follow their tracks 'til we got close enough to hear them bawl. Five and a half hours later, just before dark, we heard Old Blackie's tree bawl almost to the bottom of Arrastra Creek in the heavy spruce timber.

By this time, it was dark, just plain black, no moon and the stars looked to be a million miles away. At last, we came over a little ridge of lodgepole timber and heard this faint bawl. I thought it was way down the mountain. Gene said, "No, they're right close." About that time, here came Old Cheese slowly up the hill to us. Those dogs had been barking so long all afternoon that they were hoarse and could hardly bark. This hoarseness lasted for three or four days.

Skippy and Ole Blackie were laying at the foot of this lodgepole pine tree and when we would look straight up it, we could see a black gob that was the cat. Gene found a spot where he could get a pretty good look at the cat against the sky and said, "I think I can get him from here."

I said, "Go ahead and try it and I'll be ready for him if you just wound him."

Well, Gene turned a shot loose and he hit the cat, knocking him out of the tree. He lit in the top of another smaller tree and it acted like a springboard, throwing him straight at me. As he went over my head, I fell to the snow and shot him as he passed over me.

I did not know if I hit him or not, so I jumped over a big downfall log the way the cat had gone. When I landed, I was standing on that cat's tail. He spun around and grabbed my legs with his claws and started snapping at my knees. As I tried to wiggle them out of his reach, I was shooting at his head at the same time, missing every shot. Gene jumped over the log and shot him in the head.

His first words, "Are you hurt?"

I said, "I don't know. My legs don't hurt but I can feel blood in my boots."

He said, "Get your pants off while I get some first aid out of the pack."

When hunting was good.

I pulled down my pants and looked at those torn up legs. It looked like when you scratch your hand on the barbed wire fence, just a drop of blood popping out of a scratch here or there. Funny what the mind can do.

Well, we sure fell off that mountain and went straight to Fanny Steele's house down Arasta Creek. When she opened the door to our knock, we were hit in the face with the aroma of fresh, hot, homemade bread. She set us out a cup of coffee and fresh bread and butter.

I have never enjoyed a meal more. Wendell came and picked us up and hauled us home. It was a full day and one I'll never forget.

We'd hunted Nevada Creek in the Helmville country many times with not much luck. People were always calling us saying a lion had killed deer close to their ranch, so we'd load the dogs and go look-see. Nine times out of ten we'd find either ranch dogs or coyotes had done the job. So we didn't do too much serious hunting over there.

Then a rancher told us that he often seen cats chasing deer across the creek and up on some open hillsides on Chicken Creek. I told him, "Next time you see a lion, give me a call personal."

A few days later Wendell and I were heading down the road just a short ways from the ranch when we met Louie. He said the night before he had seen three mountain lions catch a deer up on that hillside. We said, "Let's go. We'll go get the dogs and snowshoes and meet you at the Chicken Creek road."

When we arrived at Chicken Creek, here was Louie and two other guys wanting to go along. We hadn't gone far up the creek when we found a deer kill practically eaten up. We circled and the best we could figure from sign was, it was four cats, at least, travelling together. All tracks showed them to be mature cats. Wendell and I figured an old tom, two females and a younger tom.

Right about here we cut the dogs loose, and did they go! Out of that drainage and over into big Chicken Creek where there was plenty of tall, twelve-inch fir, mighty tall trees.

We were travelling fast as the snow was only four or five inches deep. Hadn't gone far when the dogs were running them by sight. You could tell by the choppy sound of their voices. Suddenly, Blackie hit that long tree bawl and the race was over, we thought. When we got to the tree, we were short one hound, Skippy. Blackie and Cheese had two cats treed.

By the time we shot those two out of the trees, we'd lost Old Cheese. He left and we could hear him barking, running by sight. I said to Wendell, "You go look for Skippy and I'll go to Cheese." We knew each one had a cat up a tree or on the run. I went to put the collar on Blackie and she jerked away and headed in Cheese's direction like a shot.

Me and Louie took off over east and soon heard Blackie bawling, "He's up this tree." You should have heard her long bawl, just like a bell on the church.

When we got to them, they had this wild-eyed two-year-old tom up a tree. If he'd a climbed higher he'd have had to borrow St. Peter's ladder. Louie shot him and we dragged him back to where the old tom and female were, sat down and had a cup of coffee and a sandwich.

After a while, Wendell and Bert came down the mountain. They had Skippy and another she cat. Skippy had seen this cat cut off from the rest when they first jumped them and she had chased it back over the ridge into the first creek we'd jumped them out of and had her treed in an old mine hole someone had dug in the side of the hill.

Wendell said, "There were two cats cut back over that ridge. I think the other one went up the mountain."

I said, "He'll still be here someplace in the morning. Let's leave these cats and go back and get our pickup, let him settle down a bit, then come over in the morning and drive up this gulch, leave the pickup here and see if we can pick him up. That way, we don't have to pack these cats over that ridge." So we went home promising to meet Louie and friends at Ellsworth's Bar the next afternoon, as they wanted to take some pictures.

Next morning, as we were driving up the Chicken Creek road, we saw this fresh cat track cross the road about half a mile below the other cats. We turned the dogs loose and in no time at all, it seemed, Blackie tuned in that tree bawl again.

We had a friend with us who had never experienced a hunt before, so we let him shoot his first and only lion.

Now we had five mature cats in the back of the pickup and three happy dogs. It was two tom cats and three females. Guess we interrupted some kind of a cat party.

We used to do this every once in a while. Most we ever got in one day was down on Blacktail Mountain. We got six in one pile. One old female was killing deer for the whole shebang.

When we got back to Ellsworth's Bar in Helmville, there was a crowd gathered and wanted to hang them all up and get them in one picture. We finally decided on the Highlander Beer sign over the sidewalk. We strung them up and lots of pictures were taken of hunters, cats and dogs. Also, a little beer was consumed.

Now the papers picked up this hunting story and Highlander used the picture in ads. Still everyone was happy.

Then along comes a guy seeking a little advancement or notoriety in some office in Helena, the State Capitol. He knew of a law or regulation of some kind of the sort that said a bar could not advertise liquor or beer

Wendell and Howard with neighbor Tom Edwards and the six cats hanging from the sign on the Ellsworth bar in Helmville.

on a sign attached to their building outside of the bar. Now if you have a sign inside the window facing out, it's O.K. Believe it or not, old Ed Ellsworth had to tear the Highlander sign down from over his door.

I'm really sorry, Ed, but that's the way she goes when a legal eagle flies by.

Howard and Marg Copenhaver upon occasion of Howard being named second inductee into Hunters Hall of Fame by Rocky Mountain Mule Deer Federation at its annual convention in Las Vegas, Nevada, June 1992.

Winter of 1949.

PRINCE & QUEENIE

One day an old Model A car drove into the yard at the ranch and out stepped a State Trapper and lion hunter. State Trappers were hired by the Game Department and their salary was governed by a point system. You'd get so many points for a coyote, points for skunk, points for bobcat and lion. Lion brought you the most points and really helped on the size of your check at the end of the month.

Well, this guy was sort of ill-kept, six months short of a bath and hadn't seen a razor for a week. He didn't have to tell you he was a trapper, you could smell it, both him and his car. Trappers use scents or lures to attract animals and it gets into their clothes, cars and you can't get rid of it.

Well, he wanted me to go with him after a mountain lion down by Greenough. He'd seen a fresh track the night before where a cat had crossed the road. It was headed for Belmont Creek on the Blackfoot River. I said, "Sure. Now, what do I need for groceries, etc."

"All you need is your webbs," he said. "I've got everything else." I grabbed my snowshoes, called webbs, and away we went.

When I opened the door on that old Model A, I was hit by a stench of hound dog perfume, rotten meat and coyote scent. Not a smell, it definitely was a stench. I gagged down my breakfast, slammed the door and kinda let it gently soak in rather than breathe it in in one gulp, at the same time getting my neck and ears washed by two flop-eared hounds that had been eating on that rotten old deer carcass on the floor.

We arrived at Sunset Hill, where the cat track was, about 4 p.m. We put on our snowshoes and he handed me Prince's leash. I said, "Don't you want me to carry one pack?" He said, "I never use a sleeping bag. I just build a fire and I've got plenty of grub in here." To myself I said, "I'm as tough as he is. If he can take it, so can I."

The snow was about two feet deep, wet and tough shoeing, but the track was hot and Prince was tugging me along, help going uphill but rough on sidehills and it sure would jerk you down steep sidehills. By now it was getting dark, just about like the inside of a cow. Chance said, "Don't have to worry about losin' the tracks. The dogs can smell them." Along about midnight Chance tied old Queenie to a tree and said, "We'll sleep a while." It's real cold now, down about zero. We got a fire going and piled on some old bark and rotten stumps. They hold fire good. We cut a few fir boughs for a pad in the snow so we weren't laying in the snow. This way we could curl up next to the fire and turn over once in a while, burning one side and freezing the other. If the night wasn't too long, a person could make it.

By now Chance had a gallon can of water boiling. He dug into his pack and came out with a bag of tea. He dumped two handfuls of tea in this can of hot water, came up with two old tin cups and a big box of Rye Crisp. He said, "A man can survive on this and not carry a big pack. Tain't too tasty, but better than nothin." I can argue about that Rye Crisp. It's terrible, and you could paint a barn floor with that tea. I can't even stand iced tea and lemon since then.

Well, daylight finally came and after five miles of steep sidehills and being jerked down by a sixty-pound hound who wanted to run after cat, we broke out on the flats south of Belmont Creek. This is a beautiful, benchy, rolling country along the Blackfoot River. On the north side of the river is Belmont and Little Belmont Creek. South of the river are these flats and rolling hills. It's a deer yarding area. They come off of the mountains on both sides and winter here, with lots of serviceberry, mountain ash and maple brush, excellent food for the deer and elk both.

This was in March while the snow was still deep. The deer trails were everywhere, padded down solid and wide. Everywhere we looked we could see deer or the flash of white tails. Our lion track disappeared in a deer trail. Now he was at least twenty-four hours ahead of us and with all of the fresh deer tracks, we could find a print just by chance once in a while or when he'd cross over to a new deer trail.

That night was a rough one as it started to rain and that Rye Crisp was sort of soggy, but at least we had fresh water to make tea with. This time I made my own tea in my tin cup. Now, I was just a young buck and used to my Ma's cooking an' plenty of it. My backbone was sticking out front where my chest should be. I was beginning to wonder about how tough I was.

The next morning we took off our snowshoes as the snow was soft and only about six inches deep down by the river. Chance said, "Let's split up and see if we can pick up a fresh track. He's got to have made a kill here someplace and is just laying low."

I hadn't gone far when I came upon fresh tracks, showing blood on the lion's feet. I yelled at Chance and he came over, looked the track over and said, "I'll turn Queenie loose by herself. There's a lot of deer here and once in a while Prince will quit the track and chase a deer if'n he sees it running."

These hounds are crazy by now, wanting to go. He unsnapped the collar and away Queenie went. She headed up the side of the mountain. She was really bawling now. She ran by sight. You could tell by the choppiness of her voice. "She's got him on the run now," said Chance. "I knew she wouldn't run deer."

That hound music was getting closer and she was almost to the river and running fast. We started that way. "He'll hit a tree in a minute," said Chance. "Hold it. She's got him. Do you hear that tree bawl?" Anyone who has ever hunted with hounds knows that sound when a dog bawls treed.

Well, we headed her way and ran into a fir thicket. The deer trail ran right through it. We were right in the middle of it when Chance said, "Hold it. He's jumped the tree and she's running our way." About that time there was a crash of brush, and by us and almost over flew this old doe deer. Right on her tail was Old Queenie. I made a jump and a lucky grab and I got that damn hound by one leg. Chance buckled on her collar and kicked her in the ribs a few times, calling her all sorts of names that were hard on my ears. He said, "Let's cut back to the river where we first saw blood 'cause that old Tom has a kill right here somewhere."

We hadn't gone far when we came across the tracks of a female and three kittens, all with blood on their feet. I think all the noise and disturbance we'd made had goosed them out 'cause they were headed for the side of the mountain for a new spot to hide. Chance said, "Unbuckle Old Prince. He's never failed." Boy! Did Old Prince turn on the gas and did he mouth it up! You could have heard him clear over in Idaho. "They're comin' back our way," said Chance.

Sure enough, they were. He was getting louder every jump. He was just over this little ridge and coming up a draw that will break out in front of us. Boy, they were running fast. "I'll turn Queenie loose to help him tree them when they come over the ridge," said Chance. He unsnapped the snap on her collar and held onto her neck. Then, out of the draw came a great big doe. Right behind came Prince and he was sure running low. Chance tried to hold Queenie, but she was gone after Prince and his doe. Chance said, "What do we do now?" I said, "I don't know about you, but I'm headed up river and straight for home. We can come back tomorrow and get them damn dogs. They'll be tired and hungry by then."

I forded the river and boy was it cold, so I built a fire to dry out my clothes. While I'm sitting there cussing Old Chance and his hounds, I heard them dogs bawlin' on my side of the river. What's going on, I think. That cat must have crossed over on this side. I looked down river and here came those hounds bawling and running and smelling my tracks. They came up to me waggin' their tails like they was glad I was human and not another deer.

I shot in the air a couple of times and soon I saw Chance wading the river. I kept the fire going 'til he got there and dried out. Then we headed up river to that Old Model A Ford. It must have been about 2 a.m. when we drove into his place in Ovando. He lived in the old Reily house on the hill back of the church. Chance said, "Might as well stay here the rest of the night. I'll run you to the ranch come morning."

Now you ain't going to believe the rest of this story, but it's the truth. When we went into this old house, I'd never seen anything like it since or before. You'll remember what I said about that Model A Ford. Well, it was a clean flivver compared to that house. He sort of kicked things out of our way. He said, "We'll sleep in here," and led me to the bedroom. I couldn't believe my eyes. His wife and three kids were already in that bed. He woke her up and said, "Turn around crossways. We've got company." She mumbled something and turned around while he was sorting out kids. He put two of the kids on the floor and said, "Just flop down there crossways with your feet over there." Then he laid down with his head at her feet.

I know I slept a little but was sure glad to get out of there when the day started to break. I quietly sneaked out of there and put on my boots and headed for the ranch hoping he'd not wake and invite me to breakfast. I'd had about all I could take. I never saw such dirty dishes, diapers and clothes. I don't know how they lived.

Chance finally got some good hounds and became a well-known cat hunter. You would have thought this would have put the big cure on me, but I got hounds and me and my brothers hunted cats for years and loved it.

WINDY PASS

It must have been about 1933 when my brother, Gene, and I were up on top of the south peak of Mineral Hill, high above Windy Pass. We were hunting for big mule deer bucks that make their home just as high as they can in rough, craggy ridges. From the top of the cliffs we could look right straight across Windy Pass to the south side. The north side of Iron Mountain forms the south side of the pass.

High up in the top is a finger of virgin spruce left by the fires with snow slides and rock slides coming down both sides of the timber. From our vantage point we could look right into the tall trees and there stood a log cabin! We could see the roof, the north side wall, a window and a porch on the east side. When we got home and told some of the older people about it, they said, "You're plumb nuts. There never was a cabin up there. Nobody could build one on the face of that mountain." There were still some elderly people living here then who had come to this country in 1886, some of the first ranchers to settle here. None of them knew anything about it and said, "You guys are looking at a big, flat rock."

Well, we knew we had seen a cabin up there so one day we saddled up our horses and rode as far up as we could, then took off on foot and climbed and climbed. It was really tough going, but we were determined to look that cabin over and see what we could find. It was a cabin alright. More like a one-room house built out of sixteen to twenty inch spruce logs about eighteen by twenty feet in size. Someone had cut all the trees and dug out the sidehill making a flat spot about thirty by fifty feet wide right in the center of that finger of tall alpine and spruce timber. High above, near the top of the mountain, was a big outcrop of rock that caused the snowslides to split and slide down each side of the timber, never coming near the cabin. Under the porch was stacked a cord of fire wood. The roof was split logs laid two deep, then about six inches of dirt,

Scenic beauty.

then another layer of split logs and eight or ten inches of dirt on top of them. The door was hewed timber and had been left ajar. The roof had sagged, resting on the door, and you couldn't move it. We went in and were shocked by what we found.

There was a rocked up fireplace in one corner, cupboards and table, a few old rusted out skillets and tin cups and plates. There were two built-in bunk beds and a crib for a baby that was hung on rawhide straps that you could swing. We found ladies high button shoes and an old bonnet. Then there were some old leather shoes for a child about three or four years old.

We also found square cans of tomatoes and tea, part of a coffee grinder. When we cut a hole in the tomato cans you could pour out the juice. It was green and I'm sure it would have given you a bellyache if you'd eaten any of it. Across the rock slide to the east we found a faint trail that led to a spring. This spring must have been a quarter of a mile from the cabin.

What this man and woman and two little children were doing up there I don't know. There's no history of a mine or anything else in that location. From our observation we believe there were two men, a woman and two children living there—mebby a hideout for some of the old road agents in the early days.

Two years ago we had a hunter on an elk hunt. He had been a

pilot for the Forest Service for many years, spotting fires, and had flown over this area many times. He'd seen the cabin from the air and asked me if I knew anything about it, as the Forest Service told him there never was a cabin up there.

This is history that intrigues me. There is so much of it around that I wish I could trace down.

Here I was just a few days later and just mebby I'd stumbled upon another possibility of who, why and when this cabin was built and used. I was talking to an elderly gentleman about the oddity of anyone building and doing so much work in such a place. He said, "I'll bet if you had of lifted out that floor you would have found the mouth of a tunnel to his mine. Also, I'll bet it was two Chinamen.

"The Chinamen used to be all through this country. They mined on Nevada Creek and the Lincoln country then, and across the Blackfoot at Caloma and on Elk Creek for gold. Many of them would find a claim or quartz lead, then they would build a cabin right over it, mining it from under their house and no one knew where or how much they had found. They could protect it from thieves night and day.

"There was no place for horse pasture up there. White men used horses or mules. Chinamen walked and carried their belongings on their back or head."

Now, I'll leave it to you. Make up your own mind. I've given it up. I'd like to go back up there someday but my legs won't let me. Too steep.

A band of elk out in the open.

AN ELK ROAST

In over sixty years of hunting and associating with hunters, both male and female, I have come to the conclusion that none of us know just what we are doing.

When we set out to hunt, we can see a bull elk, buck deer, bear or goose of extreme size. We have in mind just such a spot where he'll be and how we'll get him. Don't tell me I'm wrong, because we are disappointed when he's not there. So we stroll along in a disappointed mood and Bang! Away goes our prize with a crash and clatter or a flash of that white tail or mebby a glimpse of a six point antler. She's all over, my friend.

So we trudge along up the mountain and there stands a two-point or spike, and we say, "This is better than none." Ker-Boom! And the mighty hunter has his game. Not the biggest but he'll sure fill the old meat locker.

I just have to tell you about my two friends, Joe and Bill. They are great hunting buddies. Along about the last of August, they said to their dear wives, "Let's go after huckleberries this weekend, mebby take the kids and camp out up Belmont Creek over the weekend." All is set and away they go.

When they get there Joe and Bill head up the mountain saying, "We'll see if there are any berries up high." Now you and I know they are scouting for game. Hunting season is fast drawing near. Ma and the kids are looking for berries, fighting mosquitoes, and trying to get a fire started to cook supper. Now this goes on one weekend after another 'til Ma and the kids have had all the berries, mosquitoes and smoke they need. Oh, yes, and hunting season opens the following Sunday.

By now all the elk and deer in Belmont Creek know Joe and Bill, not only by name but smell and footsteps. Joe has his bull spotted on that low ridge between the upper forks of Belmont with a nice harem of cows and calves. He's bugling his head off and, "I'm sure he's a six-pointer," says Joe. "Every time I come up here he's bedded on that hogback between the forks of the creek in that little swampy area. I'll be there by daylight Sunday and hang him on the meat pole." Bill says, "I got a bunch over on little Belmont, but he's only a five by four and pretty wild. Saw some good bucks, though. Heard a big bull up high on the ridge between the two upper forks. Think I'll try for him."

Now, the night before the season opens, Joe called Bill. "Kids are all sick. Don't know if I can make it early in the morning. You go ahead and I'll see you up there someplace."

Now, as Bill drove up the road, he thought to himself: Poor old Joe. Someone else will sure get his bull before he ever gets there. I think I'll swing around that way and mebby, if I have my truck at the end of the ridge, they won't come up after Joe's elk. Anyway, I can go up the ridge then swing across and bypass that bed grounds.

Up the ridge goes Bill, but the closer he gets to Joe's spot the shorter one leg gets, causing him to always angle off toward the bull's bed ground. He just can't walk straight. His left leg just pulls him always toward the sacred bed grounds. Now he's getting awful close. "I'll just check and see. I wouldn't shoot Joe's elk."

Whoa! Up jumps a bull elk right out of the brush, a five by six, not a big six-pointer. Before Bill knows it, up comes the rifle and BOOM goes the shot and away goes the bull. Bill cusses himself for spoiling poor Joe's hunt, but goes on to look for blood. Sure enough, there is the telltale streak on the ground. After him goes Bill, just like a hound on a fresh rabbit track.

Down into Little Belmont goes the bull and Bill, then up the other side clear to that rocky hogback. Here the bull drops into the center fork. It's thick dog-hair fir and old slashings and downfall. It's getting late and still no shot. Suddenly, there he was in between those big downfall in the creek. Bill administers the coup de grace and he has his bull, or Joe's. Now, the problem of getting him home. "I can't ask Joe to help me so I'll have to go back to town and get some help." Bill heads for town and help.

Four hours later Bill and his friends are stumbling over brush and downed timber, climbing up to the elk. It is raining now and flashlights don't give enough light. By daylight they have the bull elk loaded and head for town.

When they hit the outskirts of Missoula, Bill stops and says, "The elk antlers are rubbing the paint off my pickup box." Well, the boys hop out and, after completely moving the elk's body so that the head and antlers show above all, they head into town. Bill seems to be a bit addled in his thinking because he knows they all live on the northwest side of town, but that old pickup ambles up Broadway to the middle of the city's business district, then south on Higgins Avenue, across the bridge, and on out Brooks Street to Reserve Street and back north to where his friends live. The traffic was bad, with everyone going to work and honking their horns at Bill, admiring his elk.

Bill didn't see much of Joe. Seemed they never got the same days off to hunt together that year, so Joe did tell Bill someone had already shot his bull that first morning and that he had seen the blood trail.

Now when the hunting season was over and the New Year gone, one day Bill says to the little woman, "Why don't you cook up an elk roast and we'll have Joe over for an elk feed. You know poor Joe never got an elk last fall." "Fine," she says, and sets a date. We'll call her Mary. Well, Mary sets to work on that meal. She's really going to show off her culinary expertise. If you really expect the most out of a good roast, you have to prepare it right. First you lay it out to thaw slowly on the table, then some good wine in a bowl, then a dash of Kitchen Bouquet, a little garlic powder, onion salt, Tabasco sauce, a dash of Worcestershire, add some Shake 'N Bake. Now mix all this with salt and pepper and the wine. This will form a paste you can rub into the half frozen meat. Let it set in a pan to drain and season for three hours. Now you rub it down good with Kitchen Bouquet, place in the oven at 350 degrees. Don't cook too fast, but slow to retain all of the juices and a nice pink center. After all, how else are you going to make it taste like a good beef roast?

Well, Joe and family arrive, dinner is served and everyone is happy having a real nice evening. Bill and Joe are discussing plans for next year's hunt. Little does Joe know he has just eaten his gut-shot elk that has been run over fifteen miles of rugged mountain country and dragged three miles to the pickup, wallered around in the pine needles and dirt by his hunting buddy who wouldn't think of disturbing "Joe's" hunting area!

Sarah.

SARAH

I had to quit guiding hunters a few years ago because my legs and back would not put up with those steep mountains any more. I still love to see people experience the thrill of the hunt and the pleasure I get out of helping them accomplish success in taking a trophy.

However, I have guided my granddaughter, Sarah, for the last three seasons.

The first season she was old enough to buy a hunting license, we hunted several times during the season. I lucked out on showing her good bucks and three bull elk, all in good range.

It was really fun teaching her how to conceal herself so the animal was least apt to see her, how to get through the timber with the least noise. She was a very good student and could really shoot a target, putting every shot where it should be.

That first year I put her on thirteen whitetail bucks and she never fired a shot.

Then one morning she had just flubbed the dub on two bucks, one a big, long-tined five point and I was about to throw in the sponge and quit. As we started to move on to another spot, I caught a movement out of the corner of my eye. I snapped around and down in an open draw were sixteen elk travelling along a game trail in one direction. I counted three bulls tagging along behind.

I grabbed Sarah and dropped down into a ravine and ran so we would intercept them as they crossed a ridge. We got there just as the lead cow was dropping over the ridge out of sight, with fifteen elk strung out behind her.

I whispered, "Take that bull in the back of the line."

Sarah aimed, took her gun down, aimed again. The bull was ready to walk out of sight. I said, "Shoot, Sarah, or I'm going to take him."

She said, "I don't have an elk license." This was Sarah's first hunting license and she did not know it was a combination license for deer and elk.

I shot the bull just as he disappeared, so at least, we got something.

Next day after school we tried it again. We hadn't hunted long when we came upon this three-point whitetail buck and some does. I said, "Take him, Sarah. Hold low because he's awful close."

She brought her rifle up and kept aiming, pulling her head back and forth, looking through the scope. Away went the buck. Just then it hit me. How dumb could I be? After all my years of guns and guiding hunters! The stock was too long for her and she could not get a clear picture through the scope.

Sarah is a real smart gal, about 4'11" tall and she has short arms. She's a very dainty, beautiful, gracious little gal as you've ever seen. Me, I have long arms and shoot a long stock on my rifles. She was using my 220 Swift in a Ruger bolt action rifle. Now, where she had lots of time to compensate for the long stock on target, she could do fine, but in the field and a quick shot she could not find a picture.

I said, "Sarah, let's go home. I know what's your trouble now. I'm going to borrow a rifle from Ted that he cut the stock off short for his daughter and you'll get your buck tomorrow."

Well, I got the gun and before daylight next morning we were in the field awaiting daylight. Just before you could see to shoot half decent, out of some willows and quaking aspen came a doe and fawn followed by a big five-point buck. They walked right past us about sixty yards into the tall grass, feeding.

As it got lighter, the grass was so tall that an accomplished hunter would have had a hard time hitting that buck. About this time, that old doe figured something was wrong and took off for the hills to the south.

I said, "Let him go, Sarah. I know where he's going to bed. We'll hunt a circle and if we don't get a shot we'll go get him this afternoon."

Over the hills and about three-fourths of a mile away, lies a big cattail and willow swamp surrounded by quakies (quaking aspen) where I knew he liked to spend the heat of the day, and it was a bright, sunny day.

We made a big circle hunting and came out high on a hillside along about 11 o'clock. I was showing Sarah where I would place her on a little ridge close to the game trail leading from the swamp to the meadow. I told her she should sit quiet and wait while I made a hike around the swamp and back to her. I expected to jump those deer out and knew they'd head for the quakies in the meadow and come right by her.

We were resting a bit when I caught a flash of the sun on the white tip of an antler out in the middle of this big flat between the meadow and swamp. I took a peek at it with my binoculars and right out in the open and bright sun lay that big old buck just looking the country over. There was no timber or cover anywhere to cover our approach.

I said to Sarah, "We'll have to go back, drop down over that ridge and make a long sneak to the end of that ridge, then sneak up on top on our hands and knees, keeping sagebrush between us and that buck.

Well, we made it to the top of the ridge and were still 500 yards from the buck and only one small sagebrush about fifty yards down the ridge.

I said, "You crawl on your belly and keep that bush between you and Mr. Buck. When you get to it, ease yourself out slow and see what you can do. Put your crosshairs on his back line and shoot because it's got to be about 375 yards away."

She made it to the bush, leveled her rifle and let go. That buck jumped up and kicked one leg. I said, "Hold higher and get him." This time I knew she'd hit him pretty solid as he took off. She fired again, hitting in front of him. He stopped and she hit him and he just dropped—clean a kill as I've ever seen.

When we got to the buck she was all smiles and the words she said were, "Nobody in my family has ever shot this big a head." I'm sure she was right.

I measured that shot and couldn't believe it. She'd hit him three out of four shots at 459 yards across that flat with a 243 Winchester. She sure proved herself and a rifle.

This year a friend of mine who is an outfitter down on the Powder River asked me to come down and hunt with him for big muleys. He's got lots of them and some mighty big heads. He runs the Twin Butte Outfitters at Olive, Montana. His name is Paul Mobley.

I called Paul and asked if it was all right to bring Sarah along. He said sure, he'd be tickled to death. So away we went.

Now Sarah plays basketball for the high school team and when I called her and asked her if she'd go with me she said sure, she'd love to go. I asked what about basketball. She said, "If we've got a game, I'll go hunting anyway."

The first day we saw more bucks than you could shake a stick at, but only one big one, and when Paul and Sarah made a sneak on him they were almost ready to look over the ridge where he was bedded when they jumped some antelope out of the tall grass. Those antelope ran over the ridge, jumped the buck out of sight when they gained the top.

This was a completely new way of hunting to me. I've heard about it but didn't realize what hunters were talking about.

Paul has 150 or mebby 250 square sections under private lease—thousands of acres of grass and farm lands along the Powder River. This land is bench land above the Powder River breaks below.

You hunt from a pickup or four-wheel-drive Jeep Wagoneer out across these rolling hills and flats. When you spot a buck or bunch of deer, mebby a mile or so away, away you go through this grass, sage and hills at forty, fifty miles per hour or more, and head those deer off before they get into the rough breaks of the river. If you don't see a buck that pleases you, go after another bunch.

It's sure different than this old boy's used to, but fun.

Well, the next morning we took off before daylight, hoping to get Sarah a good buck before noon as Paul had a group of hunters coming in from Wisconsin that afternoon, and we wanted to get home and out of his hair.

We were in the Wagoneer when Paul spotted this big bunch of deer and said, "There's a good buck in that bunch."

Away we went across this big flat about fifty miles per hour trying to head that bunch away from the breaks, when something gave an awful jolt, like hitting a big rock in that tall grass.

Paul couldn't steer that old buggy. He stopped and we looked it over. The right front spring had broken, leaving the frame to drop down and stop the right front wheel from turning. Well, we got that rig off the hill and down to some buildings, found a couple two by fours, jacked up the front end and run them over the axle, wired them in with barbed wire, and headed for the ranch.

Here we changed to a pickup and headed out to a new area.

We were driving down this old road and came around a hill and there was a bunch of deer up on the hillside in the tall grass, one smaller buck, and as we watched, up out of the grass stood this big old boy. I took one look and said, "There's your buck, Sarah," and stepped out of the pickup and handed her her gun.

Now the grass was so tall you could only see the top of his back and his neck and head. He was about 400 yards off. She laid that rifle across the hood of the pickup and touched it off. When that gun cracked, that buck hit the ground. He was six points on one side and seven on the other and about twenty-nine-inch spread, with heavy black beams.

One nice shot and a nice trophy. "Thank you, Sarah. I enjoyed it more than you did." Also, "Thanks to the Mobley family."

We drove 1,050 miles looking for this buck. At the same time, Mike, one of Steve's guides, called his brother, who lived down there and asked him to come up here and hunt elk for a couple of days. Now this kid and Mike started up Lake Mountain, one on one ridge and the other up another at Madison Creek and ran into a huge old muley buck and shot him not far from the road. He was an old brushpile, as we call nontypical heads. Just what Sarah and me were looking for. This just proves big heads are rarely hunted for. You've got to be in the right place at the right

Sarah and her mule deer buck.

time. The skill of hunting is in the making the best of the opportunities.

I've stressed what a good rifle shot Sarah is and I'm sure you will agree with me after seeing her picture that she's going to run Cupid out of business if she ever picks up a bow and arrow.

Stair Step Trail in the wilderness.

TARPON FISHING

A number of years ago I got a phone call from an old guest in Florida. He and some friends had made a couple of fishing trips with me and Steve into the South Fork of the Flathead.

They were a jolly bunch and all chewed "Red Man" chewing tobacco, so you had to watch out or you'd get sprayed when in close contact with them. They were experts in the art of dryfly fishing—had won honors in the fly fishing contest for tarpon and bonefish in Florida.

We camped on Youngs Creek the first night, a twenty-four mile ride. The next day no one seemed interested in riding on down to the big river that day so they fished Youngs Creek and caught it on one of its best days, when you can't help but catch lots of cutthroat trout up to three and one-half pounds. It was a wonderful day. They had a great time fishing and riding the trails of the South Fork, Youngs Creek and Danaher Valley, then out over Monture Pass to Ovando.

Well, I said, "Good to hear your voice, Gary. What can I do for you?"

Now this was late in November and we had just come in from a hunt that day. We were leaving on the last hunt of the season in two more days.

Gary said, "Can you find a hole for me to go along? I'd like to try this hunting bit and get me a bull elk."

I said, "Sure, Gary, if you can get a plane to Missoula right away. I'll go to Helena and get you a license and pick you up in Missoula day after tomorrow. You find out about the plane and call me back."

Gary got the plane and I got the license and picked him up in Missoula and headed for home.

I should tell you Gary is a fishing guide in Florida for tarpon, bonefish and so forth. He lives in Islamorada and one of the best at getting big and lots of tarpon and bonefish.

As we were turning off the highway into Ovando and my home, he said, "By the way, what's this going to cost me?"

I said, "Now I'm a horse trader and, whether you know it or not, you've just traded horses. Marg and I will be down there on your doorstep come March to catch a tarpon or two."

He said, "Fine and fair enough. Don't make any motel reservations cause you'll stay at our house."

It had been a mild fall as far as weather. Just about right for good hunting. Well, Old Man Winter settled in on us that first afternoon and really gave us a blast that night. The next morning it was 26 degrees below zero and about knee-deep snow.

We were looking at the thermometer and Gary said, "I'll warm it up," and poured some hot coffee on that little glass tube. The red stuff hit the top and glass and mercury flew all over poor Gary and in his coffee.

Later that afternoon he and his guide came upon two bull elk sparring with each other. Gary shot his bull in 26 degrees below zero weather. He insisted the bulls were not fighting, just trying to keep warm. He was happy as a June bug on a sunny afternoon.

Well, the hunt turned out great.

Now it was Marg's and my time to give our part of the deal a try. We got our air tickets and drove to Missoula March 13th and climbed aboard that big sky buggy. We were on our way to spend our first vacation in sunny Florida.

In Minneapolis we changed planes. After running three miles carrying suitcases down hallways, we finally found the right aisle and walked on board that 707. I'm sure my mouth must have flown wide open from surprise. Was this thing going to fly? It was more like walking into the lobby of the New York Central Station. I never knew planes could be so big and there were people everywhere.

Well, everything went well and we sailed along, headed for Miami. It was night-time now and if you looked out the east side ports you could see a full moon rising. If you looked out the west side you could see the sun set on the western horizon. It was great for an old country boy. Unbelievable!

We hit the runway at Atlanta and were rolling down the runway when we came to a screeching halt. There we sat in the middle of the runway. After about a half hour, they unloaded all the people going to Tampa. Then we heard some pounding and thumping under the plane. This kept up for another long while. Finally, the hostess announced that all passengers going to New Orleans should disembark.

Now that left twelve of us on board headed for Miami, and the pounding increased under our feet. The speaker system came on and the pilot said to make ready to fly. Our problem was minor. The hydraulic

Marg and her trophy tarpon.

landing gear had stuck and didn't allow it to work all the way, but be assured they had it fixed as we would be in Miami in a short time.

You can bet your last dollar this old boy did not enjoy that part of the flight. I'd a rather had a horse. I knew how to land off of them.

We landed fine, picked up a Hertz car and were in Islamorada at Gary's house in no time at all. Their house was right on the beach and you could look out over the Keys at the Atlantic. It sure was different.

Next morning, March 15th, our wedding anniversary, we were in a boat headed across all that water looking for tarpon. You don't just find water and start fishing for tarpon. You go out and hunt for them. They travel in schools and you can see them from a long way off. As they swim along, they will raise their backs out of the water, then dive back down.

At a long distance it looks like a spot where the wind is rippling the water. Every once in a while you'll see a dark back showing.

The technique is to get in front of them before you start fishing. You use a live bait with a bobber up your line about two and one-half feet. As the fish you're using for bait swims around, the tarpon makes a strike, you set the hook with three hard jerks, the bobber flies off and the battle is on.

The water is not over ten feet deep and the tarpon spend a lot of time jumping and running on your line. What sport! Sometimes they will come out of the water eight to ten feet high. Standing on their tail, they will skim across the water so fast you can't believe it. Then they throw themselves sideways and when they hit the water, there is a splash fifteen to twenty feet high, and he's gone off another direction. They can run out 100 yards of your line on a run faster than I can write about it.

I was about forty-five minutes landing mine—a nice sixty-five pounder.

Marg hooked her's down by the Five-Mile Bridge just before dark one night.

Now I neglected to say that when you hooked a tarpon, the guide would throw the anchor rope, which had a buoy attached to it so you could find it again, start the motor and take after that fish because you could not hold him. Your line would break.

Anyway, this cockeyed tarpon on Marg's line headed out to sea under the bridge and towed us out into the Atlantic. It was getting dark so Gary got a powerful light and tried to keep it on that fish. When the light hit him, his eyes would shine green and bright red. After a hour and forty-five minutes of this spectacular fishing, Marg had him alongside the boat where Gary could gaff him. She had landed a fish, 105 pounds and six feet one inch. What a trophy!

We had it mounted and it takes up most of a wall in our front room.

This was for sure the best horse trade I ever made. Surely would like to find another horse trader so's I could go fishing again sometime.

Now you talk about guides knowing their country, Gary sure knew his water trails and fish.

A GUEST TALKS

MY MOST UNFORGETTABLE HUNT
By Arthur Whitney

My name is Arthur Whitney. I live in Flint, Michigan, and for many years have had a desire to go west on an elk hunt, but being tied up in the heating and air conditioning business, it was hard to find time to get away until my son came into the business with me and it gave me the time I needed for a western elk hunt. To some people a trophy sheep is number one in America, but to me elk is the number one big game trophy.

Now that I had the time, I set out to find an outfitter to hunt with. I decided I would hunt as one man to one guide, and after reading several articles in various sports magazines, I decided on the state of Montana.

In the spring of 1973, I corresponded with seven different outfitters, names taken from advertisements in magazines. In my correspondence and from materials received, I decided to let Jack Atcheson of Butte, Montana, line me up with a good outfitter, as he, being a taxidermist and hunter, would know where the good trophies come from. Finally after phone calls and letters of communications, Jack lined me up with the Howard and Steve Copenhaver Outfitters in Ovando, Montana, and through correspondence with Howard, I found out he had a September 15th to 24th opening and we would be hunting in the Bob Marshall Wilderness area. I was advised of the various equipment to bring and to come a day early if possible. I was also advised there would only be two hunters in camp at one time. The other hunter turned out to be Dr. Tom Rawls of Pompano Beach, Florida. Also, I was advised to get myself in shape, having never been out West, and I also had not ridden a horse for more than forty years. Also, the fact that I was fifty-nine years old, I had some riding practice to do.

The day finally came when I boarded a plane in Detroit,

destination Missoula, Montana, where I was picked up by Howard and taken to his place in Ovando. There I met Steve and Mrs. Copenhaver, and the next day I also met my tent partner, Tom Rawls, who flew in from Florida. I would like to say here that he (Tom Rawls) was one of the finest fellows I ever bunked with. Also, I don't believe there is a better outfitter in Montana than the Copenhavers. They have top quality horses, mules and tents, and the food was just like downtown New York. You name it and they had it.

The next day we loaded the horses, mules, the saddles and our equipment into the trucks and drove as far as we could to the wilderness area. There is no motorized equipment allowed in this area, not even a chainsaw, so everything goes in either by back-pack or horses and mules. This was the 14th of September and after unloading and saddling up and loading the packs, we were on our way to camp, which was a five or six hour ride. On this day there came up a real wet snow and we faced it all the way to camp, and with my slicker packed away in my duffel bags, I got real wet and miserable. Finally arriving in camp with the cook already there, we had a hot cup of coffee which was always ready for anyone passing through. We helped unload the packs off the mules and took our gear into the hunters' tent which consisted of two single beds with mattresses, and places to hang our clothes, and also a wood burning stove. The floor was leveled off and had an old carpet on it. The cook already had a fire in the stove so we dried ourselves off and got set for the opening, which was the next day, the 15th of September. About 5:00 a.m. on the 15th we could hear the cook preparing breakfast. At the same time, the guide was out saddling the horse, getting ready for the hunt. After we finished our meal we fixed our own sandwiches. There was plenty of apples, candy bars and oranges if we wanted them for along the way. The way we hunted, we rode out just before dawn to a selected area for that day, then tied up the horses and would hunt the mountain sides and tops, working back around to the horses by almost dark, stopping every now and then to bugle and glass the mountain meadows.

Steve was my guide. He was a tall, lanky young man of about twenty-two, and he knew the mountains like I knew the city. He took me out to one of his favorite spots, looking and bugling for a bull elk. After about an hour and a half, we tied up the horses and started sneaking up and around the mountains, stopping every so often to glass, bugle and listen. We had about six inches of wet slippery snow from the day before and it was real hard walking, especially for a greenhorn like me.

We saw several signs, tracks, and trees scrubbed up by the bull's antlers. Around noon we stopped to eat a candy bar and sandwich and to rest, so we glassed the area around us, and looking down below I saw my first bull elk in the wild. I pointed him out to Steve and after looking him over with our glasses we saw he was a large bull with seven points on each side. He had been lying down on an open hillside and had spotted us, but we were both out in the open and there wasn't any way we could get close enough to get a shot. We estimated him to be 600 yards away and I was carrying a 308 Winchester, which I knew would perhaps only cripple him at that distance. Also, the guides won't let you shoot unless they are reasonably sure you can hit and kill the animal.

Steve tried to bugle him closer but all he did was come to a pine tree about thirty feet closer and rip it to shreds with his enormous antlers, bugling most of the time while he was doing it. I had a pair of 9 x 35 binoculars and he sure looked big. When he threw his head back to bugle, his antlers about hit his rump. After about twenty minutes of this he finally decided to take his harem of nine cows and calves with him and move up into the mountain. He sure was a beautiful sight, sending his harem before him in single file and following behind them, in no hurry whatsoever.

Steve said to me, "We will wait 'til they get out of sight and we will finish climbing to the top of the mountain and come up behind them. That way, perhaps we can get closer to them." He had a general idea where they would bed down.

Finally we started our climb up and around the mountain. It took three hours to get to where we wanted to go. We came up over the top to a small bench and stand of pines where Steve figured they would be bedded down. Sure enough they were in there but they must have winded or heard us for we hadn't gone into the pines very far when we heard a noise of the elk moving and I rushed out to an opening over a narrow ridge only to get a glimpse of this big bull going into a thicket on the other side with his cows with him, only about fifty yards away, but no chance for a shot whatsoever.

We followed them in the snow for about a mile and finally had to quit and make our way back to the horses. By that time it was getting dark and the first day of hunting was over. This day sure stirred my hopes of getting a good bull. When we got back to camp we found the other hunter, Tom, and his guide, Howard, had not seen anything that day.

The next day was pretty much the same routine in a different area. We had bulls bugling and very close to us in the thickets. So close that we could hear them scrubbing and raking the trees with their antlers, but they would not come out into the open so I could get a shot, or see what they were as far as a trophy.

When we got back to camp, we found a happy hunter there. Dr. Tom Rawls said that about 9:00 a.m. that morning, Howard had three bulls bugling right close together and finally called one out into the meadow on the hillside and Doc got him. He was a real nice perfect five-point bull, estimated to go around 900 pounds. Doc had been trying for several years to get a bull elk and he was sure happy with this one. So was I. I would like to say here that I am a hunter and am not disappointed if I do not get any game. I have hunted whitetail deer in Michigan since I was a youngster and have taken over forty bucks, some real nice trophies.

The next day we went into the area where Doc got his bull, hoping the other two would be somewhere in the neighborhood. By this time the snow was gone and we could not even get a bugle. They had moved out of the area. While hunting to the top of this mountain we saw fifteen mule deer bucks, some of them real good heads which looked to be in the thirty-inch class, but wanting to get a bull first I didn't even think of shooting one. After getting back to camp we told Howard and Doc about the mule deer so they went up in there the next day to see if they could find a good trophy, but as the elk had moved out, so had the bucks we saw. They were nowhere to be found, although while they were in the area they saw two large bull elk fighting, so they told us that night and the next day Steve and I were on our way to see if we could locate them.

The weather closed in on us and we got up to where they had been spotted and had to wait for the fog to lift. After it got so we could glass the hillsides all we saw that day was two cows. Now it was getting late in the hunt so I decided if I was going to take any meat home, I would shoot a good mule deer if we came upon one. The weather was bad most of this time and the bulls stayed in the heavy timber. With but two days left to hunt we went into another area that day and in the afternoon we came upon a nice five-point buck, so I took him. He made a real nice mount and the meat was real good and tender.

The morning of the last hunt, Howard told me if I didn't get my bull that day he would make arrangements for me to come back and hunt later if I wanted to. They were real disappointed that I had not been able to get a shot at a bull. This day was also a futile day so this was the end of my 1973 elk hunt. I was not disappointed, Steve had done his very best but the bulls would not cooperate. I saw a lot of beautiful country and had taken a real nice muley so I told Howard I was real satisfied with my hunt but would like to come back the following fall of 1974. He advised me to take the second hunt, a fourteen day hunt which would give me more time. He lined me up for this hunt to start the 29th of September, 1974.

The first thing I did when I got home was to purchase a .338 Winchester magnum rifle, which if I would have had this the first day of my first hunt I could have shot that seven-point bull.

Well, after much practice with my gun and some horseback riding, the last of September rolled around and I was on my way back to Montana looking for that big bull, as no one had taken him in 1973, although the record bull taken in Montana in 1973 was by a hunter hunting with Steve and Howard in the same general area that I saw the big one, but he was a real large six-point.

I was picked up at the airport in Missoula by Steve and we were on our way to Ovando. The next day the other hunter by the name of Boris, a Lieutenant Colonel in the Air Force from Tucson, Arizona, arrived, so we loaded our gear in two pickups and was on our way to the mountains. As this was the second hunt, Howard already had made a corral to keep the horses in and all we had to do was pack the mules and saddle our horses and we were on our way. The two hunters on the first hunt had taken nice five- and six-point bulls and a mule deer so I really had high hopes of getting mine this hunt.

The weather was real good this hunt. The coldest it got was about 22 degrees above zero. Arriving in camp we got our gear unloaded and rested up for the next day when the hunt would begin. This was a fourteen-day hunt which would only give you twelve days of actually hunting, for we had one day riding in and one day riding out which counted as the hunt. The hunt in 1973 was wet and real nasty, this hunt in 1974 was just the opposite. It was real bright moonlight and clear days so the bulls were coming out in the meadows at night and doing their bugling and staying in the thick timber in the daytime, so we had to sneak hunt, trailing and glassing for them all the time.

We would get on a fresh bull track and trail him up in the mountains and down in the heavy red willows around the creek beds, only to get about fifty yards from him and hear him go crashing out ahead of us with his antlers really crashing the brush as he went through them. One day Steve saw one running in the pines ahead of us and we took off as fast as we could, hoping to get where we might see him cross an opening so I might get a shot, but he was too smart for us. He stayed in the thick pines. We went back to where he came from and found out that he had been standing and looking at us from a clump of pines for quite a while.

When we started to hunt on the first day, I told Steve if I got my bull that year I had a feeling it would be in the general area I saw the big one in the 1973 hunt. We did quite a lot of stalking and lots of climbing and trailing, but I found that a good bull elk is very elusive—about like the whitetail deer. One day we trailed four large elk for almost a whole day and came upon them in a thicket where I got a good look at them. There was a fair sized bull in the bunch but I could not get a good look at the antlers because he kept his head down and was in between the cows, so I had to pass him up.

One night we stayed real late until dark and was a long way from camp, knowing that the moon would come out bright and it wouldn't be hard riding back because we were about eight miles from camp. We saw many signs and thought we might see them moving around. We got at a vantage point where we could do a lot of glassing and sure enough, just before dusk, we saw an elk come out of a thicket, walking toward us. We put our glasses on him and found him to be a young spike bull, although he was quite big, but he wasn't what I was looking for. It was getting close to the end of the hunt and I hadn't seen the bull I wanted yet, although we had seen twenty elk, of which four were bulls, but none that I was satisfied with. I had decided I would go right down to the last minute, hoping to get a good trophy.

Finally came the last day of the hunt, Friday, October 12, 1974, and we would have to pack out the next day. While talking to Howard that morning, as he was doing most of the cooking and had hired his son-in-law, John, to guide the other hunter, he said to me, "Art, you are a good hunter and I can't understand why we haven't been able to get you a shot at a good bull. If you don't get your bull today I want you to come back down and rest up with us for two days, call your wife and tell her you will be home when you get there, and I'm going out with you myself and we will hunt until you get your bull no matter how long it takes." I told him I appreciated this very much and that I might take him up on the offer, but that I still have one day to hunt and still have plenty of time to get a good bull, as I never give up, realizing the last hour of the hunt is just as good as the first.

We saddled our horses and got ready to ride out for the final day. I asked Steve where we were going to hunt and he said, "Where you said you thought you would get your bull, in the area where we saw the big one the first day of the 1973 hunt."

Now comes the main reason I am writing the story of my hunt. Not to take anything away from Steve and Howard and their outfit, for I believe they are the finest people and guides in the West. At least I believe there aren't any better. I am a Christian and believe in God and His Holy Word. One place in Psalms it says, "Trust in the Lord and he shall give the desire of thine heart." and Jesus said, "If you ask anything in my name I will do it." So I prayed to God as I was riding out that morning, that last day that he would fulfill this desire I had in my heart. I said, "Lord, I know that I am unworthy, but you are my Heavenly Father, I am your Son redeemed by the sacrifice of your Son, Jesus Christ on the Cross, and I am asking for a nice trophy bull."

We tied up our horses around the general area we had before and started our last day of hunting. We had hunted until about noon and had seen some fresh signs but no elk. It was starting to get late in the hunt now, only about seven hours left so just before noon again I prayed to God and said, "Like a little child I believe what you said in Your Word and I am still asking and believing You will fulfill this desire I have in my heart to get a nice trophy bull."

About noon we came to a small meadow on the mountain side. We

We became friends.

could see quite afar in the area and we sat down on a log to eat a sandwich. After we were almost through eating, Steve said to me, "Art, look down there, way down around the creek bed." There was a single elk walking real fast across a small opening. We did not have time to get our glass on him and being so far away we couldn't tell whether it was a cow or a bull. We became alerted and got prepared in case he should change his mind and come up the mountainside.

In about fifteen minutes a large mule deer buck cut across in front of us and Steve and I decided that it being noon-time, something had scared it out of its bed so we got up and started sneaking around the mountainside from where the deer got up. We had not travelled more than 200 feet around the bend and there stood the most beautiful six point bull that any man could want.

The minute we saw him, Steve dropped to the ground in front of me and said, "Art, there he is, the one we are looking for. He is a good one, take him." I don't believe it took me more than two seconds to get off a good shot. He was only about 100 yards away. My first shot hit him real hard but he fell on his face and then got up and was half falling and stumbling down the mountainside, so Steve told me to hit him again. I shot him again and he folded up and rolled up against a pine tree thicket. When I got down to where he lay, the first thing I did was say, "Thank you,

Art Whitney and bull.

Lord, in answer to my prayer."

Steve also mentioned that I must have someone up above working for me and I told him I sure did. There is no doubt whatsoever in my mind that this was the elk we saw down in the creek bottom and God had changed his course and brought him up to me where I could get a shot at him. He was a very large bull, a six-point with heavy beams and large tines. My guide estimated he would go 1,050 pounds. Also, he was what was called a travelling bull, going from herd to herd, fighting off other bulls. This we could tell by the tips of his antlers where they were nicked and a large cut was across his nose where he had been raked by another bull.

Now we had the problem of caping him out as I wanted a shoulder mount. Then the drawing of the innards and cleaning him out, and cutting pine branches to cover him up to keep the birds out. I believe we were about five or six miles from camp so Steve carried the cape back to the horses as we were afraid a grizzly bear might destroy it if we left it overnight. He threw it over his saddle and rode on it on the way back to camp. When we got back Howard was out in the corral getting things ready for the ride out the next morning. When he saw us coming in early, about 4:00 p.m., he surmised what had happened and he walked out to meet us. When he heard what had happened and about the good-sized bull and saw the cape, I think he was almost happier than I was. This was the night to celebrate, but I'm not a drinking man, so I settled for a can of pop.

That night two friends of the Copenhavers rode in to take some pictures of the Wilderness Area. They agreed to go out with Steve and me the next morning and take pictures, and help skin out my bull and quarter him so we could pack him on the three mules we took with us to carry him out.

They call Montana the Big Sky Country, but I called it God's Country. I don't believe there is a prettier place in the United States than up on top of the Continental Divide in the Bob Marshall Wilderness.

When we got up at 6:00 a.m. the next morning we rode out with the pack mules up the mountainside where my elk was. We quartered him and loaded him up and was on our way back to camp. The other hunter, who was unsuccessful, his guide and Howard, were already on their way out and we made arrangements for Howard to meet us around 6:00 p.m. with the pickup truck at the corral. I would like to mention here that the horses and mules that Steve and Howard have seemed to be able to climb like goats. They would climb where I could hardly climb.

We stopped at camp, ate a sandwich and had a cup of coffee. Then we were ready for our long ride out. Altogether that day I believe we rode between twenty-eight and thirty miles and I was sure one stiff but happy hunter. Finally we made it to the trucks and Howard congratulated me on getting one nice set of antlers.

That night Mrs. Copenhaver had a lovely dinner for us. About 9:00 p.m. Steve loaded my equipment, the cape and antlers in his car and I went into Missoula where I had a hotel room waiting as I had to catch a plane home at 10:00 a.m. I brought my cape and antlers home with me and had them mounted by Hilde in Clarkston, Michigan, and I just got the mount back about the middle of May. I also would like to say—while I am writing this I am lying in a hospital bed recuperating from a heart attack and I don't believe I will ever be able to go back in the mountains hunting again.

In conclusion, I would like to thank the State of Montana for the fine game management program they have there and the privilege of hunting in their great state. I would like to thank the Copenhavers for their very fine family and all out effort they put out to get a person an elk.

I would most of all like to thank the Lord for my trophy bull and my most unforgettable hunt.

What makes an outfitter.

AN OUTFITTER IS BORN

Along about 1951 my wife gave birth to a son we named Steve. A little blond-headed guy with a loud voice and an empty stomach.

He grew fast and quick—liked to ride horses and at the age of four years wanted to go in the hills with me on every trip.

One day I was taking a party into Meadow Creek on a five-day fishing trip. It wasn't too long a ride so I said he could go along on his horse, Bobby. He made the ride fine and the guests really enjoyed this little guy.

After supper the first night when everyone was getting set up for the night I put up a tepee tent and spread Steve's and my sleeping bags in it. He couldn't wait to get in that sleeping bag. He'd never spent a night in a tent before, let alone back in the mountains.

When I got ready to bed down I showed him how to take care of himself should Mother Nature call in the night. He should crawl out of his sleeping bag, slip on his boots and go out the door and let nature take care of what was needed.

Now along about 3 o'clock in the morning I awoke with a start and there was Steve standing up piddling right on my sleeping bag. He'd followed directions to a tee but missed the door. He sure livened up that camp next morning when he told the guests what he'd done.

Shortly after this Marg, Steve, Susie and I were in the car headed for Missoula. Marg had been taking the kids to Sunday School and teaching them about the Bible. Out of a clear blue sky Steve said, "Howard, do you remember Methusela?"

A year or two after this Marg and I were building a new home on the ranch and as everyone finds out the cost was getting too high for our pocketbook and we were having our problems about raising some cash.

Well, I took Steve on another trip in the hills with another party. We were camped in an area where you had to watch your horses or they'd

Why I had to make a living.

head for the Danaher. Someone usually slept on the back trail and made sure that they didn't head back at night. You'd take your sleeping bag behind your saddle and sleep along the back trail. If the stock came down the trail you'd shove them back toward camp. Then in the morning you'd pick up your sleeping bag and tie it behind your saddle and wrangle the horses back to camp by daylight.

Well, I was going to sleep on the trail this night and Steve wanted to go with me so I said, "Sure," and away we went.

When we got to this place in the trail along the river where the horses couldn't get by, we spread our beds and rolled in. It was a nice moonlight night and we were laying there resting when Steve says, "Howard, I wish we lived right here. Then we would have no worry about money and building a house." I said, "How come? We'd still have to have a house." He said, "Oh, we could just cut down some of these trees and build one ourselves. Don't need no money for boards and stuff."

Now a few short years rolled by and Steve was riding a little

Morgan saddle horse. This was a small horse but full of fire. It seemed you never saw Steve that he and Toby were not on a run. I wondered if Toby ever could walk. He was tough. The biggest little horse I ever owned.

Now Steve had a cousin Bruce who was the same age and he rode a horse named Brownie. One day they decided to hook Toby in harness to an old buggy we had at the ranch and take their sisters for a buggy ride.

Well, Toby would have nothing to do with that four-wheeled cart so the boys decided to try Old Brownie. Brownie stood right still 'til they had him all hooked to the buggy. Brownie was a real gentle horse but when Steve slapped him on the fanny and said, "Get up," he went up alright. About thirty feet to the jump and out across the meadow.

When they hit the first irrigation ditch Bruce bailed out. Steve was doing fine pulling on the reins and hollering, "Whoa! Whoa!" When another ditch got in the way they lost the hind wheels off that buggy. Also, Brownie lost Steve at the same time. Now Brownie had the front wheels, shafts and front seat to himself. In another circle around the meadow and a couple of barbed wire fences he lost the whole buggy and half his harness.

When the boys caught up to him he was in the corral with his head in the feed rack munching hay just like nothing had happened. Every once in a while when haying you'd find part of that old buggy or a piece of harness and have another good laugh.

By the time Steve was in high school he would work for me all summer dragging ten mules on pack trips and holding his own with the other men—a top hand and a good packer. He could do anything needed to be done on a pack trip into the mountains, an excellent flyfisherman, knew the trails and understood game and was learning to hunt.

By the time he'd finished high school his desire was to be a mechanic. So off to automotive school he went. He graduated and could fix anything that was greasy and make it run but the mountains drew him back and he's still here, a top outfitter and one of the best elk hunters I know, with a deep concern for his guest and a knowledge of the mountains and its game developed by a lifetime in the hills. It's many the happy guest that he's had the privilege of outfitting and guiding.

I must tell you about some boys from Missouri who have hunted with him many times. There was Warren, Dave and others who hunted deer, elk and antelope. One year seven of them went antelope hunting, had a ball, shot up a lot of ammunition and returned four days later with twenty-two antelope, as I remember, then headed for the back country and bull elk. They did fine and came out with some small six-point bulls.

Now these were plumb nice heads but Warren and Dave were looking for something closer to record book heads. They hunted their hearts out and their legs off but no such luck.

When they left for home Steve asked them to come back the last few days of the season and he'd help them get a big mule deer buck as the mule deer would be in the rut then. When the rut comes on the big boys come off the tops of the mountains and out of the thickets. Late season has snow and you can spot them easier.

Well Dave was the only one that could get away so Steve told him to come on. Steve and Mike, a guide, took Dave on horseback up on Ovando Mountain, tied their horses and climbed to the top of a sharp ridge where they could glass for bucks.

While Steve and Mike are glassing a bunch of does across a deep ravine hoping a big buck would show up, Dave is sitting behind them taking a little rest. All of a sudden there is a loud snap. Once you've heard it you'll know what it is. It's someone firing a rifle with no shell in the chamber. Both Steve and Mike wheel around and there stands Dave with an empty gun in his hand and that big six-point bull elk waving his tail goodbye as he plunges out of sight over the ridge. Dave said, "Forgot to load my gun when we got off the horses."

Now last fall they both came back. "We'll get him this time for sure." Hunting was real tough. Nothing seemed to work. They'd spot a big bunch of elk at long range and before they could get close enough some old lead cow would spot them and give a warning bark and away'd go the bulls and the boys would strike another zero.

Steve and Dusty and Spooks.

Steve found this big bunch of fifty-some elk and four bulls in the East Fork canyon and all of them decided to make a try the next day coming in from three directions—three guides, Steve, Tim and Mike with three hunters. Now I'm the cook and offered to give them a skillet and coffee pot but they told me to just have plenty of chow ready by dark.

Well this Old Boy cooked up one of the best meals I've ever cooked—pies, roast and all the trimmins. Along about 10 o'clock me and the extra guide ate supper by ourselves. I kept supper warm 'til 2 o'clock and gave it up.

Next morning I made up some lunches and had Rich take his saddle horse and lunches and head to the top of the mountain where I knew the boys would leave their horses before stalking those elk. Along about 2 o'clock that afternoon here they came—what a noisy crew and wanting something to eat! I said, I sent you lunches." "That was fine," they said, "but we want breakfast." So I fixed them bacon, eggs and hotcakes and were they full of stories.

It seemed they made their stalk but the elk had moved and they all met on a hogback ridge, sat down and were deciding what's next and glassing the country below them. Steve spotted an elk coming over a ridge about 600 yards away. Soon there were fifty-eight cows and calves and nine bulls on that hillside. I believe they said there were five big horned bulls.

They made their sneak and gained another 150 yards closer but it was all downhill and steep. The elk spotted them again so they had to shoot at extreme range. Each hunter picked the bull he wanted and shot and shot. No luck and the elk are still there for this coming season.

When they started back up that steep mountain they just didn't have the steam left in them to make it. They built a fire near the creek and spent a real nice miserable night out—no coffee, no supper, no bed, just one side burned and the other side froze. By morning their muscles were set up like cement and it took them 'til noon to get back to their saddle horses. Then a two and a half hour ride back to camp where a grey-haired cook was drinking coffee and laughing all to himself.

Dave bought a 338 magnum and said, "I'll get him this fall." You better plan on helping him, Warren, because every year makes that mountain steeper and higher.

Taking a lunch break along the trail.

Friends.

BILL BROOKS

Bill's first hunt was a dandy. We had beautiful weather. It seemed Old Man Weather was doing his best for us. It was beautiful in the daytime and gave us a nice wet four to six inches of snow every other night or so. You can't ask for anything better during the early rut season. It's cool enough to keep those old bulls happy and bugling.

Bill was in a group of four hunters from Pennsylvania, all of them young and ready to go. The first morning I took Bill and his hunting partner up into Hell's Half Acre, a heavy-timbered area, open sidehills on the south exposures, nice big timber. On the north exposures it was thick timber and lots of big downfall, thus its name.

Well, we hunted along up this half open ridge, new snow and not a track on it. It sure didn't look good and I was wondering if I should find a new area to hunt. We'd started from camp about daylight and it was now 10 o'clock and not a sound or track. We had just stopped and were sitting on an old log when across the creek and on top of the high ridge to the south, came this long, keyed bugle of a bull looking for cows.

I answered him to get his location better fixed in my mind for the stalk. It was going to be tough getting down to the creek and up to the top of that ridge with all that thick fir and spruce thickets and downfall. It also was as steep as a church steeple.

While I was mentally picking a route, that bull gave me another bugle and he seemed closer. I came back at him and beat a stick on the log. Did he ever come alive! Bugling and ripping trees with his antlers. He was hot to trot. I kept teasing him, hoping he'd come part way at least.

All of a sudden you knew he was on his way, bellering and slapping little trees as he came through those thickets and down the hill. I could get a glimpse of him every once in awhile so I placed my hunters, one up the hill to my right and had Bill set right beside me. That way we had two different angles to watch for him when he hit our side of the creek

The China Wall.

and started up a big game trail leading to where we sat.

It seemed like five hours, but it was just a few minutes 'til I saw him emerge from the timber and cross the creek, starting up this game trail straight at us. He had a big, symmetrical set of six-point antlers. He was beautiful and floating along so smooth and easy.

Bill couldn't see him, although he was out in the open on this trail, mebby 200 yards away. Just as Bill saw him, he stepped behind a big yellow pine and the branches hid him and he stopped. I figured, "Oh! No! He's picked up our scent or our partner has moved and he's seen him!"

We waited. He waited. The adrenaline had built up in poor Bill 'til I thought he was going to explode. I eased my bugle up and gave a blast, all I had. He let a bawl out of him and came up that trail on a trot, straight at us about 100 yards away.

Bill was on him and turned one loose and he had a trophy any hunter would envy in any man's camp.

Well, I caped him out and we field dressed him and covered the carcass with fir boughs to keep the eagles off him. Then we hunted on over to Canyon Creek and back to camp, seeing some muley bucks on the Canyon Creek hills, but nothing big.

When we got to camp, Steve and one of the other hunters had got a nice six-point down on the bench on the Dry Fork.

It was a lively camp that night.

The next morning we went to pack Bill's bull out. He was helping me.

After I had the meat all quartered and mantied up, I led the pack animals down the steep hill to the elk and stopped them on the game trail where they had good footing. After loading the first one, I took it up the hill and tied it to a tree.

When I went to lift the last quarter on this old mare, she started to back up. I said, "Hold her, Bill."

Well, Bill dropped the lead rope and grabbed the halter on each side of her head with both hands, jerking the sides of the halter up over her eyes. She rared up and rolled down that hill. I only had the downhill side loaded so the weight tipped her over and she ended up down the hill with all four legs under a big old deadfall tree. What a mess! I accused Bill of trying to kiss her and she wanted no part of that.

I had to chop the log in two with her fighting to get up, as Bill wouldn't hold her head. He'd had enough of this added entertainment. Finally, we got her out of there and back to camp in time for supper.

The next day was another good one for fresh snow, just right. I had found sign of a large bunch of elk on the Canyon Creek hills the day we got Bill's elk, so Bill, Eric and I headed for Hell's Half Acre again.

We were lunching out up on top by a big elk wallow when I tried my bugle. Right back came an answering bugle. He was down on the Canyon Creek side, but real close. I moved over to the edge of the ridge and gave another bugle. Two bulls answered me less than a hundred yards away. They were down over the edge in a ravine.

Before I could think of what to do, this old cow came running out of the ravine, headed for the wallow. Right behind her was the big bull and right behind him came two more and a bunch of cows and calves. Eric slammed that old rifle to his shoulder and down went the lead bull, right where we left our coats and lunches.

The elk just kept coming out of that draw and over the ridge into the Dry Fork side and heavy timber. All in all, there were thirty-some cows and calves and four big-horned bulls.

Eric's bull was seven on one side and eight points on the other. Awful long beams.

You talk about some happy hunters, they were it.

This is something I never had happen to me before or after in all the years of elk hunting. The two following hunts that year, my hunters took two more bulls in exactly the same spot. If you had drawn a circle around the spots where they fell, it would not have been 100 feet across, and all three of them nice bulls and happy hunters.

Now, if any of you pilgrims want such an experience, just call Steve at 406-793-5547.

Bill and friends hunted with us several different times. On his last hunt he left this little note on the kitchen table where I found it on the next hunt. I'm sure you will enjoy it.

PENNSYLVANIA PILGRIMS IN MONTANA

As folks in ole Montana say,
  Ne'er came a good hunter from PA.
They can't walk as far or go as high
  And, plainly speaking, just get by.
So try to beat what we did get
  For you three we two will surely bet
Your favorite brew, whatever it be,
  Cause we did have a shooting spree.
Two bulls a 'hangin' and a black bear blue,
  Two bucks missed, and a nine inch billy seen too.
And if you plan a trip this great,
  You'd better be in the best damn shape,
For it's been said in the Copenhaver Camp
  That whether it be fair, cloudy, or damp,
Mornings you climb right from your tent,
  And all day long you continue your ascent.
And when day is done, and the sun doth simmer
  You climb back to camp to have your dinner.
Happy Sore Asses, Blisters, and
Above All HAPPY HUNTING!
    --Bill Brooks and Sam Weiss

WHAT A GUIDE SHOULD NEVER TELL
OR ONE GUIDE'S SIN

Of all the outfitters I know, I have undoubtedly been one of the fortunate, even mebby the MOST fortunate, guys ever in the business.

When you work with many different people from all walks of life, you can expect some rank ones. I can probably count on one hand those people I would only pack into the mountains once. Never again.

Hunters, fishermen or just plain sightseers, even if they don't know what they are doing, are willing to listen and learn and enjoy what's going on. That's what they came for in the first place, to have a good time.

But, once in awhile there is someone we can't understand. The old saying goes, "Why not smile and make everyone love you instead of working so hard to be obnoxious."

This person was one of those offbeat old heifers I'm going to tell you about. If she happens to read this and recognizes herself, I'll feel I have really done a good job of writing about her and mebby it will help some other poor lad.

We booked this guy, Larry, and his wife, Mary, on a special goat and elk hunt. I was guiding and Marg, my wife, was cooking and acting as a lady companion for Mary.

When they arrived we learned that Larry was a small man who, in World War II, had his lungs shot up. Consequently, he only had one lung and other injuries that slowed him up pretty bad. He was quiet, gentlemanly and a very likeable guy, the sort of a guy that any guide would work his heart out for and overlook all shortcomings.

Now Mary hit you with a blast of hot air and "I know everything" attitude. It didn't take her five minutes to let you know she was the hunter and she'd probably have to kill game for Larry if he got any. Her words were, "He's no good at home and worse in the mountains." It seemed Larry couldn't even blow his nose without her telling him to.

Why we have game laws.

At first, I thought this guy must not have any guts at all to let her belittle him all the time. Personally, I'd have bounced her on her fanny if she talked to me like that. Now Larry paid no heed at all, it seemed, and I figured he must think she'll have a heart attack and lay down and die, then I'll kick her behind a rotten log and enjoy life.

She was a small woman, no fat, just sinew, steel and miserable. She had a sharp face with a long hook nose in front. If it had been a few years before, I would have called her a "cherry picker." She could have hooked her nose over a limb and picked cherries with both hands.

Anyway, as we headed down Willow Flats past Limestone I was foolish enough to stop and show them some mountain goats up on Apex Mountain. She stated emphatically, "Me and you will go get a billy tomorrow. Marg can take care of Larry."

The next morning, early, all four of us took up the trail for Limestone and the goats. When we got up to Limestone Lake, I left Larry and Marg at the lake with the saddle horses and said, "Let's go, Mary."

Well, I figured I'd cut her down in size before we made the ridge behind Apex Mountain. No matter how hard I climbed, Mary was right behind me, not even puffing. She was a tough old girl. I'll give her credit for that much.

When we topped out and finally got a good billy spotted, he was about 500 yards away and we couldn't get any closer. Mary was shooting a 270 Winchester. Now a shot like this can be made, but you'd better be a good shot and have a lot of luck.

Mary shot and she shot. All that old billy would do was walk over to where the last bullet had hit, smell the spot and look around. He was enjoying it as much as I. Finally, after eighteen shots Mary said, "My scope must be off. Let's try it another day."

She was really shook up about missing. As we went down the mountain we came into a rocky ravine and out the other side went another billy about 100 yards away. Mary threw up that rifle and missed two more times. Out of shells. I'm sure she was so mad about missing the first one, she never put the crosshairs on this last billy. She just shot.

When we got to the horses, she started in on Larry. "I'd have got that goat if you'd have let me take your rifle." She could not accept any self blame. It was always poor Larry's fault.

On the way home, I spotted another billy up on Danaher Mountain in what we call the Big Scoop, a rocky basin just under the top. I told them how I could get Larry in close up there, but she wouldn't have it. It was her goat and just her and me were going after it. Larry and Marg could stay in camp.

I'm going to tell you something. This old boy was getting mad. I'd had it with this gal.

Next morning the four of us rode out again. When I came even with the big snowslide under the Scoop, I tied the horses, left Marg and Larry to have a day to themselves, and headed up that mountain. I never looked back at Mary. I did not try to hit easy going. I just poured on the gas (all I had) right up to the tip top of Danaher.

I never even looked for that billy. I just said, " He's left," and down the mountain I went. Mary's having a little trouble keeping up at this point. I paid no notice, just headed for the horses. When we got there Mary said, "We got time to go up on Apex again?"

I'll tell you I felt like killing someone but couldn't make up my mind whether it should be her or me.

As we rode back to camp, we got quite a ways ahead of the girls. Larry said, "Howard, every time we go hunting she shoots all the game and then we go home before I have a chance to get mine. I'm sick and tired of it. I wish, just for once, I could shoot something."

I said, "Larry, why don't you tell her to go to hell and do what you want?

He says, "I don't know. I just can't be nasty."

I said to myself, "I could. Real easy, too."

We rode down Willow Flat where the trail winds in and out along the edge of the meadow, little hogback finger ridges coming down into the meadow from off of Concord Mountain, leaving a little draw every 200 yards or so. The trail we were on went in and out of these swales.

As we rode along, I heard a bull elk bugle up on the mountainside. I stopped and listened. After a bit, I was sure it was a lone bull headed for the meadow ground looking for romance.

I said, "Larry, stay here," and rode back to meet Marg and Mary back in the swale we'd just come out of.

I said, "You guys stay right here and watch that game trail on that hogback 'cause a bull is coming off the mountain. Larry and I will watch the next trail up ahead." I tied the horses behind some trees and rushed back to Larry.

I hid our horses and picked a good spot and started bugling that bull in. I figured he was a loner and would come down our trail with a little coaxing. He sure did. He came out of the timber above us right on the trail with his nose in the air and looking for a girl friend. Old Larry leveled on him and made a clean kill. He was a very nice six-point with long tines.

Larry said, "Can we leave in the morning?"

I said, "You bet."

Next morning I sent Marg, Mary and Larry up the trail for the ranch. Mary wasn't speaking, and I guessed why.

I packed up their gear, picked up the bull elk and caught them before they reached the ranch.

We loaded all their stuff and elk in their station wagon and as they drove off, old Larry winked at me.

Mebby you'll say I was rotten mean but I don't feel that way. Poor Larry passed away the next winter and I'll always figure he died happy with my help.

NEW YORK

    This old boy never was much of a city slicker, but I found out when Marg and I took a trip to Springfield, Massachusetts, in the later 50's, that I could stand some learnin'.

    We had an old Chrysler Airflow car and drove. I had an awful time with cars passing me at seventy or eighty miles an hour on a two lane highway. About the time we hit Minneapolis, I was doing all right and had my speed up to sixty-five miles per, sometimes seventy, just like the rest.

    They were building a freeway through Minneapolis to Chicago, and that's where trouble started. The road was well signed right into the center of the city. There it stopped and every street I turned into said ONE WAY with arrows pointing straight at me. Finally, I got out of there after driving up and down every street in west Minneapolis.

    I thought I had it made 'til I got to Chicago and got on the expressway going east toward New York. I never dreamed there was so many cars and trucks all going the same way at eighty miles an hour, eight lanes going each way and no place to hide.

    We finally got off it and done good 'til we came to the George Washington Bridge in New York, and here were those signs again, ONE WAY, DO NOT ENTER, no place to go. I finally saw a hole in the traffic and pushed that Old Chrysler across four lanes and into one going across the bridge.

    When we got across the bridge, the traffic was so thick I couldn't turn up the Parkway north so I mosied up a road that parallelled it, thinking there'd be a crossroad back to the freeway. No such luck. We got up on a little hill and I could look down and see the parkway and a sign pointing to Springfield, Massachusetts. Between us was a gentle slope down to the road. I swung that old car off the road and down the hill to the parkway. Well, when we got down there, there was a rock wall along the road about two-feet high. I drove up along the stone wall looking for a place to drive down into the barrow pit and back up on the parkway.

Pretty soon I saw a little shack with a light shining in the window up along this grassy-like meadow. I drove up and got out and knocked on the door. An old guy opened the door and you should have seen the look on his face when he saw me and my car parked in front of his door.

He yelled, "How the hell did you get here?"

I said I drove down from the road above and wanted to get on the parkway.

He kept yelling. "You're driving over dead people. This is a graveyard." He wouldn't tell me how to get out to the parkway—just, "You're driving over dead people."

I gave it up, got in the car and drove along 'til I found a place I could tear some rocks out of that wall and jumped the old Chrysler off into the barrow pit. When the traffic gave me a chance, I gunned that old girl and we were headed north on the parkway. Just like as if we had good sense.

Well, we finally got to Springfield and found the little rural town that Marg's relation lived in and figured we'd done great, no extra road expense. That old Chrysler ran like a dream. Now this was one of those old cars that had a soft top on it made out of a material like a raincoat. When we got up next morning, I looked out and there lies a damn goat right on top of my car. When I went out to chase him off, he couldn't move. All four feet had pushed through the roof and hung down inside the car.

We finally lifted him off the car and, I'm telling you, that roof was not moisture proof any longer. After driving all over Springfield, I found an upholstery outfit that could put a new top on it. It cost me $14.50. I'd hate to see the same bill today.

Well, we took another highway back to New York. Sure was pretty country, only too many people. When we got to New York, we came into a big circle sort of driveway where all the roads came together. Now, you were supposed to drive around this circle 'til you came to where your road turned off and scoot out right.

Well, I couldn't see any that didn't say DO NOT ENTER. Finally, I saw one and made a dive up it. I was doing fine, but had to drive between two streetcar tracks. All of a sudden Marg says, "That policeman is blowing his whistle at us, I think." By this time I saw we were following a streetcar and down in a big ditch.

That cop was running along the sidewalk up above blowing his whistle and waving his arms.

Marg rolled the window down and the cop hollered for us to turn up the next loading ramp where the people boarded the street cars. I did this and he was there to meet us and show us how to get back on the road. I

World Fair Centennial Train—New York 1964.

couldn't get any directions out of him on how to get out of that fair city. He just kept telling me to go right now. I did and went the wrong way again.

Now, by this time we were looking for a dinner bucket and saw this sign, Greenwich Village Restaurant. I backed that old car over and pulled up in front.

When we got inside to eat, you wouldn't believe it only by seeing it. I had never seen so many strange characters all dressed different in my life, and hairdos that were unbelievable.

One character I'll never forget. She had what looked like her underwear on with this huge floor length fur coat and bare feet. You never saw such getups called clothes. When I asked people later about it, they would start to laugh and say, "Well, you can tell people you have been to Greenwich Village, New York." It sure beat Frisco at that.

FAMILY

Friends, at this point of the game in writing this book, I feel I cannot close it without expressing my feelings for family. Like it or not, I still have to do it. Without a family I would not have had anything to write about.

It seems to me in this day of economic, social and professionalism, along with divorces, that the family unit is taking a beating.

I come from a large family of eight. We learned to fight, love and help each other at any time. Us boys had black eyes and bloody noses, and the girls learned to be ladies, hold their own in a fight, and become leaders with dignity and poise.

I can look back now and see where our parents may have overlooked some things but always demanded honesty, fairness and decency.

It's like an old man told his sons one time, "I don't care what you become in your life, be it a banker, preacher, or garbage man. Just be the best garbage man in town."

Economics of today govern a large family but what I gained from one I feel is lost by those not experiencing these values.

The first was a girl, Leona by name. She had no thought but for others 'til she passed away at the age of fourteen years.

Next was Gene who had the disposition of a bulldog when it comes to right or wrong, and a doer.

I was next with the makeup of an alarm clock wound up tight, who had trouble keeping his feet on the narrow trail.

Lawrence was number four with the bullheadedness of a Hereford Bull in fly time. Once he got pointed, he had no trouble following a straight trail the right way.

Number five was a beautiful little girl, Louise, with a voice like a bird and fingers that could drag music out of an untuned piano. You

The Copenhaver clan in a photo on the home place taken about 1937. From left, Wendell, Dad, Louise, Lawrence, Mom, Betty, Howard, Leon and Gene.

should have heard her sing. She was a graceful lady but don't ever think she couldn't uphold her end in a brawl with us boys.

Well, now, Wendell was the sixth. When he was made, they threw away the dies. Oh, he has a temper, is a musician and perfectionist, and is loved by all who know him.

Number seven was Leon, with an inborn sense of honesty, enthusiasm, drive and deep love for his family, work and the great outdoors. He'd rather fish than eat.

Now came Betty, a beautiful, ambitious gal who has dedicated her life to teaching "learning disabled" children. She's got to be a certain kind of person. You should have heard her and Louise harmonizing with singing. I call her a "Dumb Blonde with Red Hair."

Thank you all for your help. Sometimes I've needed your push.

If it hadn't of been for this big family of hungry mouths and my habit of being late for dinner, I would not have been hollow from the skull

The Copenhavers at a family reunion in 1986. Standing from left, Lawrence, Wendell, Leon, Gene and Howard. Kneeling, from left, Betty and Louise.

down and would not have had anyplace to store all these memories.

Now, many thousands of years ago there was a big pile of rocks and dirt, piled up in a big mass. It was called North America.

Upon this high mass lived horses, cows, elk, buffalo, and man with all other wildlife, trees, grass, flowers and birds. All were happy and life was easy. If the winters were cold or the summers too hot, it made no difference; they just went along and did the best they knew how. Then someone invented reproduction and soon this old rock pile was in a turmoil.

Someone had to do something to straighten it out. Some guy started screaming "more education," another claimed new industry would solve our problems. So education and industry developed, all the time pushing us poor people farther away from the basics of life—always striving to better ouselves and this pile of rocks.

It is like one environmentalist said the other day, "Wilderness is nothing more than a decaying piece of country left to its own destiny."

Another fellow, trying to explain how wrong he was, used this as an explanation. Every year the automobile companies try hard to please you by building a car that suits your desires and you are never satisfied. Now a horse, an elk and wilderness have not been changed for many hundreds of years. A horse is still just a horse—nothing else. We, as people, have forgotten our basic, and fundamental, way of life.

I, for one, miss the things that were so simple when I was young.